THE
ANCIENT
GREEKS

Other titles in the *Lost Civilizations* series include:

The Ancient Egyptians
The Ancient Romans
Empires of Mesopotamia
The Mayans

LOST CIVILIZATIONS

THE ANCIENT GREEKS

Don Nardo

LUCENT BOOKS
P.O. BOX 289011
SAN DIEGO, CA 92198-9011

On Cover: The Parthenon atop the Acropolis, Athens.

Library of Congress Cataloging-in-Publication Data

pm

Nardo, Don, 1947–
   The ancient Greeks / by Don Nardo.
      p. cm. — (Lost civilizations)
Includes bibliographical references and index.
Summary: Describes the rise to power of ancient Greece, its glorious empire, its
civilization, and its eventual decline.
   ISBN 1-56006-705-5 (hardcover: alk. paper)
   1. Greece—Civilization—To 146 B.C.—Juvenile literature. [1. Greece—Civilization
—To 146 B.C.] I. Title. II. Lost civilizations (San Diego, Calif.)
   DF77 .N374 2001
   938—dc21

                                                                    00-008760

Copyright © 2001 by Lucent Books, Inc.
P.O. Box 289011, San Diego, CA 92198-9011
Printed in the U.S.A.

Contents

FOREWORD

"What marvel is this?" asked the noted eighteenth-century German poet and philosopher, Friedrich Schiller. "O earth . . . what is your lap sending forth? Is there life in the deeps as well? A race yet unknown hiding under the lava?" The "marvel" that excited Schiller was the discovery, in the early 1700s, of two entire ancient Roman cities buried beneath over sixty feet of hardened volcanic ash and lava near the modern city of Naples, on Italy's western coast. "Ancient Pompeii is found again!" Schiller joyfully exclaimed. "And the city of Hercules rises!"

People had known about the existence of long lost civilizations before Schiller's day, of course. Stonehenge, a circle of huge, very ancient stones had stood, silent and mysterious, on a plain in Britain as long as people could remember. And the ruins of temples and other structures erected by the ancient inhabitants of Egypt, Palestine, Greece, and Rome had for untold centuries sprawled in magnificent profusion throughout the Mediterranean world. But when, why, and how were these monuments built? And what were the exact histories and beliefs of the peoples who built them? A few scattered surviving ancient literary texts had provided some partial answers to some of these questions. But not until Pompeii and Herculaneum started to emerge from the ashes did the modern world begin to study and re-construct lost civilizations in a systematic manner.

Even then, the process was at first slow and uncertain. Pompeii, a bustling, prosperous town of some twenty thousand inhabitants, and the smaller Herculaneum met their doom on August 24, A.D. 79, when the nearby volcano, Mt. Vesuvius, blew its top and literally erased them from the map. For nearly seventeen centuries, their contents, preserved in a massive cocoon of volcanic debris, rested undisturbed. Not until the early eighteenth century did people begin raising statues and other artifacts from the buried cities; and at first this was done in a haphazard, unscientific manner. The diggers, who were seeking art treasures to adorn their gardens and mansions, gave no thought to the historical value of the finds. The sad fact was that at the time no trained experts existed to dig up and study lost civilizations in a proper manner.

This unfortunate situation began to change in 1763. In that year, Johann J. Winckelmann, a German librarian fascinated by antiquities (the name then used for ancient artifacts), began to investigate Pompeii and Herculaneum. Although he made some mistakes and drew some wrong conclusions, Winckelmann laid the initial, crucial groundwork for a new science—archaeology (a term derived from two Greek words meaning "to talk about ancient things.")

His book, *History of the Art of Antiquity*, became a model for the first generation of archaeologists to follow in their efforts to understand other lost civilizations. "With unerring sensitivity," noted scholar C. W. Ceram explains, "Winckelmann groped toward original insights, and expressed them with such power of language that the cultured European world was carried away by a wave of enthusiasm for the antique ideal. This . . . was of prime importance in shaping the course of archaeology in the following century. It demonstrated means of understanding ancient cultures through their artifacts."

In the two centuries that followed, archaeologists, historians, and other scholars began to piece together the remains of lost civilizations around the world. The glory that was Greece, the grandeur that was Rome, the cradles of human civilization in Egypt's Nile valley and Mesopotamia's Tigris-Euphrates valley, the colorful royal court of ancient China's Han Dynasty, the mysterious stone cities of the Maya and Aztec in Central America—all of these and many more were revealed in fascinating, often startling, if sometimes incomplete detail by the romantic adventure of archaeological research. This work, which continues, is vital. "Digs are in progress all over the world," says Ceram. "For we need to understand the past five thousand years in order to master the next hundred years."

Each volume in the *Lost Civilizations* series examines the history, works, everyday life, and importance of ancient cultures. The archaeological discoveries and methods used to gather this knowledge are stressed throughout. Where possible, quotes by the ancients themselves, and also by later historians, archaeologists, and other experts support and enliven the text. Primary and secondary sources are carefully documented by footnotes and each volume supplies the reader with an extensive Works Consulted list. These and other research tools, including glossaries and time lines, afford the reader a thorough understanding of how a civilization that was long lost has once more seen the light of day and begun to reveal its secrets to its captivated modern descendants.

HOW DO WE KNOW ABOUT THE GREEKS?

One of the most famous of all the world's lost civilizations, that of the ancient Greeks, is also one of the best documented. This probably comes as no surprise to those who have seen photos or drawings of Greek ruins and especially to those who have been to Greece and witnessed firsthand its enormous number of ruined ancient structures. Among the most popular are the remains of the magnificent Parthenon and other temples atop Athens's central hill, the Acropolis; the vast theater at Epidaurus, so well preserved that plays are still produced there; and the atmospheric sanctuary and Temple of Apollo at Delphi, where the famous oracle once foretold future events. With their cracked stones huddled, still and silent, under the warm Mediterranean sun, these and other remnants of a vanished culture seem to beckon to the visitor. On this very spot long, long ago, they seem to say, people lived and loved and dreamed, just as people do today.

These impressive ruins also hint that Greece, which is today a small nation of modest means and influence, was once the home of a culturally splendid civilization. And in fact, scholars have determined that it was one of the *most* splendid, as well as one of the most influential, civilizations in world history. The ancient Greeks, who called their land Hellas and themselves Hellenes, left behind a remarkable and momentous cultural heritage. Their art, architecture, sculpture, political ideas, social and military customs, literature, philosophic and scientific ideas, and language have come, in profound ways, to shape the cultures and ideas of all later Western (European-based) lands and peoples.

Yet these facts have not been revealed by ancient ruins alone. If the remains of the stone walls, temples, theaters, and other ancient structures that have laid aboveground for centuries were the only evidence available about ancient Greece, historians would know little for certain about this long-lost civilization. The colorful and fascinating picture we now have of ancient Greek culture has been pieced together from several different kinds of evidence, some of it literary and some of it archaeological in nature.

The literary sources consist of surviving documents written by Greeks, Romans, and others who lived in ancient times. Some are histories, such as those by Herodotus, a fifth-century B.C. Greek who wrote about the peoples and customs of that century; Thucydides, Herodotus's younger contemporary, who chronicled the Peloponnesian War, which proved disastrous for many of the Greek states; and Xenophon (ZEN-uh-phon), who in the fourth century B.C. described some of the major political and military events of his own time. Other important written sources include the surviving works of Aeschylus and the other great fifth-century B.C. Athenian playwrights. Though their plots are generally fictional and their characters larger-than-life or satiric, these works often capture or reflect contemporary social mores and religious beliefs. The treatises of philosopher-scientists—most notably Plato, Aristotle, and Theophrastus (all fourth-century B.C. Greeks)—cover a wide range of subjects, ranging from politics and government to religion and morality. Of additional value are several surviving speeches from the Athenian law courts. Composed by professional writers and orators for average citizens pleading their cases, these reveal not only much legal information, but also numerous facts about everyday life. And last, but often not least, are the commentaries of later ancient writers, such as the first-century A.D. Greek biographer and moralist Plutarch and the second-century A.D. Greek traveler Pausanias. Fortunately for future generations, they were prolific writers who had access to sources now lost and/or described sites and buildings that no longer exist.

The ruins of the Propylaea, a massive entrance gate with wings that extend forward, grace the western flank of the Athenian Acropolis, the chief symbol of the glories of ancient Greece.

A large part of the archaeological evidence for ancient Greece consists of ceramic containers, such as vases, cups, and storage jars. Pictured is a rhyton, or drinking horn, fashioned in the shape of a ram's head.

Supplementing these literary sources is information unearthed by archaeologists, scholars who dig up and study the remains of past civilizations. Among the many kinds of archaeological evidence are inscriptions (words or symbols carved or etched, usually into stone); bones, tools, weapons, jewelry, and other artifacts from graves; the remains of houses and other recently excavated buildings, along with their contents, sometimes including remnants of furniture and personal items; trade goods, storage jars, and other artifacts found in shipwrecks; coins, found in excavated buildings or ships or in hordes buried in the ground for safekeeping; and

pottery, paintings, statues, and other works by ancient artisans and artists. Each of these types of artifact makes its own unique contribution to the overall picture of Greece's lost culture.

One particular kind of inscription, for example, the tomb epitaph, is valuable because it reveals information that most other sources do not, namely the lives and feelings of those who had no political power or voice—women, children, and slaves. (The vast majority of written sources were composed by men and describe the lives and deeds of well-to-do and famous individuals, mostly free adult men.) "Chaerestrate lies in this tomb" reads an epitaph found at Piraeus, Athens's port town. "When she was alive, her husband loved her. When she died, he lamented."[1] This is one of the few existing pieces of evidence that at least some Greek husbands and wives, whose marriages were almost always arranged, actually loved one other.

The most abundant and perhaps the most versatile kind of archaeological evidence illuminating ancient Greek history and life is pottery, including bowls, cups, cooking pots, storage jars, decorative vases, and so on. As noted archaeologist and art historian John G. Pedley explains here, pottery, whether whole or in pieces, not only reveals information about Greek society and customs, but also helps excavators to date the sites in which the pottery was found.

> Pottery breaks easily but is not really destroyed entirely and survives in the earth. . . . Since making pots from fired clay was the commonest craft in antiquity [ancient times] and since pots had many uses—for cooking, eating, drinking, for storage, and for offerings in [religious] sanctuaries and tombs—pottery provides the largest category of archaeological evidence that has survived . . . and is invaluable evidence for social history. The uses to which it was put are studied, as well as its painted scenes depicting customs, beliefs, and rites. How the wares were distributed, trade connections and patterns, tell us about economic history. Then it can also tell us about its evolution as an art form. Such are the quantities which have come down to us, that scholars have been able to work out the stages of development of various shapes and systems of decoration, and have been able to relate these stages to historically recorded events. Accordingly, pottery has become a critical tool for dating archaeological contexts, and for dating buildings or objects by stylistic analogy.[2]

Combining and carefully correlating the literary and archaeological sources is an enormous job that keeps thousands of scholars constantly busy. But these efforts have proved fruitful. Using traditional techniques worked out in the early twentieth century, along with more recently developed research tools, such as aerial and underwater photography and computers, archaeologists and historians have managed to construct a reasonably accurate and sometimes vivid account of the ancient Greek saga. In these ways, a civilization long lost is being recovered, bit by painstaking bit, and the opening in a vital window to the past continues to widen.

CHAPTER ONE

PALACE-FORTRESSES AND WARLORDS: GREECE IN THE BRONZE AGE

The first advanced human cultures appeared in Greece in the historical era that modern historians call the Bronze Age (ca. 3000–ca. 1100 B.C.), so named because its inhabitants fashioned their tools and weapons from bronze, an alloy of copper and tin. People did inhabit the region long before the Bronze Age; however, for many thousands of years, they were primitive hunter-gatherers who used stone tools and eked out an impoverished seminomadic existence. Not until about 6000 B.C. did permanent settlements sustained by agriculture and raising livestock arise. And only in the Bronze Age did the local inhabitants begin erecting stone structures and cities and establishing small kingdoms.

The first such cities and kingdoms in Greece were built by the Minoans (named by modern scholars after the legendary Cretan king Minos), who inhabited Crete and a few other southern Aegean Islands. Although they apparently did not speak Greek, they created the first highly civilized culture on Greek soil and came to exert a powerful cultural influence on the area's first Greek speakers. Scholars re-

fer to this second group of early city-builders, who settled the nearby mainland, as Mycenaeans. The name comes from their chief fortress-town of Mycenae, whose imposing ruins still crown a rocky hilltop in the northeastern Peloponnesus (the large peninsula that makes up the southern third of Greece).

Both of these early peoples passed away and entered the realm of legend long before the advent of the later Greek states that produced the famous Pericles, Socrates, Aristotle, and Alexander the Great. But vivid, if often distorted, memories of the "proto-Greek" societies lingered and became the basis for many of the myths that enriched later Greek religion and literature. As the classical Greek city-states eventually emerged and established settlements throughout the Mediterranean world, their inhabitants looked back with a mixture of fascination and awe at what they called the "Age of Heroes."

Minoan Wonders

Archaeological evidence shows that the relatively rapid development of the Minoans'

12

splendid civilization began shortly after 2000 B.C., when they started building large "palaces." These probably served various communal, administrative, religious, and ceremonial purposes in addition to housing the royal family. Eventually these structures became huge, multistoried, and richly decorated. Some, like the largest and most famous one—at Knossos, near Crete's northern coast—even featured early versions of flush toilets and hot and cold running water, advanced facilities that would not be seen again in Europe for a great many centuries. The Minoans appear to have practiced a collective form of agriculture. The state (run

by a king and a group of aristocrats) controlled and exploited the herders, farmers, and laborers, who were mostly of modest means. The Minoans also had many ships with which they carried on a prosperous trade with a number of Egyptian and Near Eastern cities. In addition, they engaged in complex religious rites and staged thrilling athletic contests in which young men and women leapt and did somersaults over the backs of charging bulls.

The world was introduced to these and other wonders of Minoan civilization thanks to the diligent efforts of a young British archaeologist named Arthur Evans. Between

The grand staircase of the palace at Knossos leads to this landing, which archaeologists call the Hall of the Guards. The beautiful wall frescoes include figure-of-eight shields.

WAS THE MINOAN EMPIRE ATLANTIS?

The story of Theseus and the Minotaur is not the only famous legend that suggests that Minoan Crete exerted some form of political or military domination over neighboring areas, including the Greek mainland. Most scholars now believe that the volcanic destruction of Thera (the entire center of which collapsed into the sea) and its devastating effects on Crete gave rise to the legend of Atlantis. This is an excerpt from Plato's *Timaeus* (Benjamin Jowett's translation), in which the character Critias quotes an Egyptian priest addressing an Athenian leader.

"Now in this island of Atlantis there was a great and wonderful empire [the Minoan?] which had rule over the whole island [Crete?] and several others, and over parts of the continent [mainland Greece?] . . . This vast power . . . endeavored to subdue at a blow our country and yours . . . and then . . . your country [Athens?] shone forth, in excellence of her virtue and strength, among all mankind. She was preeminent in courage and military skill, and was the leader of the Hellenes [i.e., Greeks]. . . . She defeated and triumphed over the invaders, and preserved from slavery those who were not yet subjugated, and generously liberated all the rest. . . . But afterwards there occurred violent earthquakes and floods; and in a single day and night of misfortune all your warlike men in a body sank into the earth, and the island of Atlantis in like manner disappeared in the depths of the sea."

1900 and 1935, he excavated and partially restored the palace at Knossos. "Decisive and determined," scholar Christopher Mee explains,

Evans knew enough of Knossus to be optimistic [about what he might find there], but even he could not have predicted how soon his expectations would be fulfilled. Within a week of starting to dig on March 23 [1900], he had found "a kind of baked clay bar, rather like a stone chisel in shape, though broken at one end, with script

on it and what appear to be numerals" that proved this was a literate society. . . . By 1905 the excavations were more or less complete, and Evans' systematic study of the finds, including superb colored frescoes [paintings done on wet plaster], elegant stone vases, and richly decorated pottery, had begun. . . . Between 1922 and 1930 he also undertook the gaily painted reconstruction of the palace, with its central courtyard, throne room, royal apartments, and pillared Hall of the Double Axes, that visitors see today.[3]

Evans dubbed the writing he had found "Linear A"; later he found a similar, slightly more elaborate script and called it "Linear B." Unable to decipher these scripts, Evans and other scholars assumed they were both written forms of long-dead non-Greek languages.

Thera and the Great Volcanic Eruption

As time went on, other excavators unearthed more buried palaces and towns on Crete and some nearby Aegean Islands. In 1967 Greek archaeologist Spyridon Marinatos began bringing to light a Bronze Age town at Akrotiri, on the small island of Thera (about eighty miles north of Crete). This settlement had been buried by thick layers of ash when the volcano on Thera exploded with awesome fury sometime between 1630 and 1475 B.C. J. Lesley Fitton, a curator at the British Museum, describes the excavations at Akrotiri and what they have revealed:

> Houses and streets—a whole section of a Bronze Age town—began to emerge from the enveloping layer of ash and pumice [volcanic glass]. The buildings were marvelously well preserved, their contents more or less as their inhabitants had left them. No people had been trapped by the destruction [as evidenced by the fact that no skeletons have been found in the ruins] . . . so it seems they had had some warning of disaster and were able to escape. Many of their possessions were left behind; even the shape of their wooden furniture was in some cases preserved as impressions in the

ash that swept into the rooms. Perhaps most exciting of all to the modern world, their wall-paintings once again came to light . . . substantially complete, and still glowing in something like their original colors. . . . First impressions of this Bronze Age town concentrated on its obvious debts to Minoan Crete. Both art and architecture showed distinct Cretan influence. Indeed, the evidence from Akrotiri often put things long known from Crete into a new perspective. Thus, while Minoan buildings on Crete were rarely preserved above a few feet in height . . . on Thera the buildings . . . were preserved to two and three stories.[4]

While Minoan Crete exerted strong artistic and cultural influences on the inhabitants of Thera, in return Thera profoundly affected the residents of Crete. The Theran influence took the form of some severe damage from the great eruption, which some scholars have called the most devastating in human history. Correlating disaster evidence from Thera with dislodged wall blocks and other evidence for destruction at various Cretan sites, scholars have determined that the eruption dealt a serious, if temporary, blow to much of the Minoan sphere. Earthquakes evidently toppled many buildings on Crete, towering sea waves wrecked many Minoan ships and docks, and a blanket of fine ash fell over a wide area, causing agricultural damage. Archaeological evidence suggests that the Minoans managed to recover from the catastrophe but that they never regained their former prosperity. It was only a matter of time, therefore, before they would fall prey to some aggressive, more resourceful neighbor.

Mycenaean Warlords

That aggressive neighbor turned out to be the Mycenaeans, whose settlements and fortresses dotted the southern Greek mainland. The exact date that the Mycenaeans' forebears first arrived in Greece is uncertain. It may have been as early as 2100 B.C. or as late as 1600 B.C., but most scholars suspect that they entered Greece from the north and/or northeast in two or more waves beginning about 2000 B.C.[5]

At first the Mycenaeans, who used the script Evans had christened Linear B, were culturally backward in comparison to the Minoans, whose society they apparently admired, envied, and to some degree copied. According to noted scholar Sarah B. Pomeroy and her colleagues, the Mycenaeans

practiced herding and agriculture, and they knew metallurgy and other crafts, such as pottery and cloth-making. Of their society we can surmise only that they were organized in families and larger groups (clans and tribes) that were patriarchal (the father was the supreme authority figure) and patrilineal (descent was reckoned in the male line). Their primary divinity was Zeus,

Though this section of a street in the Bronze Age town of Akrotiri, on the island of Thera, sustained damage in the great eruption, some storage jars still rest in their original positions.

a powerful male god; and they were a warlike people.[6]

The mainlanders may also have come under Minoan military domination for some undetermined length of time; the Minoans did, after all, control the Aegean Sea lanes and could have imposed their will on weaker neighbors. This situation may be the basis for the well-known Greek myth of Theseus, in which Cretan overlords periodically demanded and got supplies of sacrificial victims from the mainland city of Athens. The young Athenians were regularly sacrificed to the Minotaur, a creature half-man and half-bull, until Theseus, an Athenian prince, slew the beast and released the prisoners. (The Minotaur was likely a garbled memory of Minoan priests, who, some evidence suggests, wore bull masks when performing sacrifices.)

By the fifteenth century B.C., however, the situation had changed dramatically. Not only was Minoan Crete in sharp decline, but the mainland Mycenaeans had become organized into several small but powerful and aggressive kingdoms. Sometime during the 1400s B.C., one or more of these kingdoms invaded Crete and took over Knossos and the other Minoan palace-centers. The Mycenaean warlords then controlled the Aegean sphere for the next two centuries, each ruling from one of several mighty stone palace-fortresses that sprang up on the mainland. The Mycenaeans "were spectacular builders," wrote the late, noted classical scholar C. M. Bowra.

Their palaces were built within formidable citadels with walls 10 feet thick, and some of their royal tombs were enormous beehive structures made of stones weighing, sometimes, as much as 120 tons. They were also im-

This nineteenth-century engraving shows Theseus slaying the fearsome Minotaur.

mensely wealthy, especially in metals, and most especially in gold. . . . In Mycenaean tombs, diggers have found death masks and breastplates of gold. . . . Decisions of the Mycenaean king and his court were carried out by an officialdom consisting, in diminishing order, of military leaders, administrative officials, charioteers, and mayors of the group of villages that surrounded the city.[7]

Archaeology Sheds Light on Mycenaean Culture

These and other facts about Mycenaean culture began to come to light in the 1870s

MYCENAEAN PALACES—SYMBOLS OF POWER

In this excerpt from his book, *The Birth of Greece*, noted French scholar Pierre Leveque describes some of the imposing citadels constructed by the Mycenaean warlords.

"Mycenaean-period palaces were . . . symbols of royal power—impregnable and forbidding. The earliest fortifications of the one at Mycenae . . . were repeatedly enlarged. . . . Over the course of the [fourteenth and fifteenth centuries B.C.] were added huge ramparts securing the spur of the hill, a monumental entrance (the famous Lion Gate), and a back gate. . . . Near the close of the thirteenth century B.C., a hideout with concealed doors was added on the eastern side, and a tunnel dug to a deep spring. . . . The arrangement of the palace at Tiryns, a few miles to the southeast, was similar. There too a vast enclosing wall was added at the end of the thirteenth century B.C., clearly designed as a refuge for people and animals in the event of an attack. Common to the design of these mainland palaces was a central series of three chambers. First came two vestibules [front hallways]—one of them with an adjoining bathroom in which guests might wash and rest—and then a large hall, with four central columns supporting the roof. This great hall was known as the *megaron*. . . . Two adjacent great halls have been excavated at Tiryns. The hall at the unfortified palace at Pylos [in the southwestern Peloponnesus] is decorated with a superb fresco depicting a young god of music."

when German archaeologist Heinrich Schliemann initiated excavation of the ruined palace-fortress at Mycenae. The site's famous "Lion Gate" and parts of some of its walls had stood visible since ancient times; but their age and meaning had long remained unknown. (Because of the great size of the stones used in their construction, the classical Greeks thought they had been erected by the Cyclopes, a mythical race of giants.) Exploring the site, Schliemann discovered elaborate graves containing golden masks, finely wrought weapons, and other valuables, suggesting that they belonged to the members of a royal family. This prompted his claim to have found the remains of Agamemnon, the legendary king of Mycenae (a claim that remains unproven).

Schliemann and later excavators also found pottery and other artifacts at Mycenae and other Mycenaean fortresses, relics that helped to date these sites and to shed further light on their original inhabitants. This was possible because some of the artifacts found were Egyptian (having made their way there through maritime trade between the two peoples) and scholars already had methods of dating Egyptian objects with a fair degree of accuracy. According to John Pedley,

> This meant that these archaeologists could now date the Mycenaean pottery using the Egyptian chronology [that had already been worked out]. Moreover, they now realized that Egyptian tomb paintings of the eighteenth Dynasty portrayed Mycenaean objects [also obtained through trade], to which approximate dates could then be given. Thus they concluded that this Mycenaean civilization had flourished between about 1600 and 1300 B.C.[8]

Although dating the Mycenaean sites helped to establish when they flourished, it did not reveal the personal nature and identities of the Mycenaeans themselves. A major revelation in this regard occurred in the 1950s when British scholar Michael Ventris discovered that the Linear B script they used for writing was an early form of Greek. This meant that the Mycenaeans were not, as previously thought, a foreign people who happened to occupy Greece before the Greeks. They were instead Greeks themselves and the direct ancestors of the classical Greeks.

The Mycenaeans and Troy

The discovery that the Mycenaeans were early Greeks also provided an added dimen-

sion to a particularly crucial and colorful event in their history, one long studied and hotly debated by scholars. This was their possible connection to the famous legend of the Trojan War. The story of the siege and sacking of the prosperous city of Troy by an alliance of Greek kings is told in the *Iliad*, an epic poem attributed to the legendary eighth-century B.C. Greek bard Homer. (Homer's other epic, the *Odyssey*, tells the story of the adventures of one of these kings—Odysseus—after the war's conclusion.) Modern scholars had long assumed that Troy and the siege described by Homer were fictitious. But in 1870 Heinrich Schliemann, who believed Troy was a real place, stunned the world by digging it up. He uncovered a series of cities built on top of one

The famous Lion Gate at Mycenae, which leads to the ruins of a Bronze Age palace.

another at a site in northwestern Asia Minor (what is now Turkey) and came to believe that the sixth city from the bottom was Homer's Troy.

Since Schliemann's time, the consensus of archaeologists has shifted, however. This is because more recent evidence shows that the city now labeled Troy VIIa underwent a siege about 1220 B.C., the approximate period the mythical Trojan War supposedly occurred. It is still not categorically proven that the war remembered by Homer, if there actually was such an event, took place at this time. But evidence suggests that the Mycenaeans prospered, at least in part, by

This bust of Homer was carved long after his death. No one knows his true appearance.

raiding the coasts of Asia Minor. And it is entirely possible that a group of Mycenaean warlords formed a temporary alliance to attack what was probably the most powerful city in the region at the time.

If the Mycenaeans did in fact sack Troy, the expedition turned out to be the most important event in their history, at least as it relates to later Greek history. This was because of the monumental importance the later Greeks ascribed to Homer's epics. They viewed the leading characters of these stories (including Achilles, Agamemnon, Hector, and Odysseus) as larger-than-life heroes who interacted with the gods in a glorious past age. In fact, most of the important ancient Greek myths originated in the Age of Heroes, now known to be the late Greek Bronze Age. More significantly, well-known scholar Michael Grant explains, the Homeric poems

> supplied the Greeks with their greatest civilizing influence, and formed the foundation of their literary, artistic, moral, social, educational, and political attitudes. . . . They attracted universal esteem and reverence, too, as sources of general and practical wisdom, as arguments for heroic yet human nobility and dignity, as incentives to vigorous . . . manly action, and as mines of endless quotations and commentaries: the common property of Greeks everywhere.[9]

Sudden Decline

The Trojan War may also have been, in a sense, the Mycenaeans' swan song. Not long after Troy's fall, perhaps about 1200 B.C. or shortly thereafter, the Aegean sphere, as well as many parts of the Near East, under-

This scene from the Trojan War is carved on the side of a sarcophagus (stone coffin). That legendary conflict was a consistently popular theme for later Greek artists and writers.

went a period of unexpected and unprecedented upheaval. Archaeological evidence shows clearly that most of the major Mycenaean strongholds were sacked and burned, never to be rebuilt. Theories advanced by scholars to explain the demise of Mycenaean civilization include civil conflicts, economic collapse, invasion by tribal peoples migrating from the north and east, and others.[10]

Whatever the cause or causes of the catastrophe, Greek civilization suddenly declined and entered a cultural dark age. As the old palaces crumbled, people became illiterate and lost many of the political and artistic skills that had supported the Bronze Age kingdoms. Not all was lost, however, for some civilized skills remained, along with scattered memories of the great heroes and other ancestors who had lived in happier, more prosperous times. It would take the Greeks who clung to these memories several centuries to recover fully; but the fruits of that recovery would, in the fullness of time, lead the Western world down a bold new path.

CHAPTER TWO

THE GREEKS REINVENT THEM-SELVES: THE DARK AND ARCHAIC AGES

Modern historians divide the roughly six hundred years following the collapse of Greece's Bronze Age society into two broad historical periods. In the first, the Dark Age (ca. 1100–ca. 800 B.C.), Greek civilization was in a sense sleeping within a cultural cocoon and quietly reinventing itself; in the second of the two periods, the Archaic Age (ca. 800–ca. 500 B.C.), it awakened and began to reach for new horizons, eventually surpassing the achievements of prior ages. New communities, called city-states, arose all over the Greek sphere—some of these states boldly planted colonies on distant Mediterranean shores—and Greek artists and architects began to develop the skills and styles that would later reach maturity in one of history's greatest cultural golden ages.

During these same years, Homer's epic poems appeared and became widely known. These works not only provided the Greeks with a link to a dimly remembered cultural past, but also reminded them that, regardless of political and other differences, they all spoke the same language and worshiped the same gods. Besides the Homeric poems, very little literature was produced in the Dark and Archaic Ages: most of what *was* produced was not written down; and most of what was written down has not survived. So the chief sources of evidence for this still somewhat obscure part of the Greek saga are archaeological —the remains of pottery, tools, weapons, houses, tombs, temples, sunken ships, and so forth.

Why the Dark Age Was Dark

Unfortunately, even archaeological evidence remains scarce for the Greek Dark Age, which is so labeled partly for this very reason; hence scholars still know very little for certain about life in this period. It also appears to have been "dark" in the sense that civilization temporarily declined during its early years. For the most part, Greek society experienced a general loss of literacy, major decreases in population (for at least the first century or so), widespread poverty, and an overall deterioration of both the standard of living and cultural standards.

These negative developments were, of course, the result of the collapse of the Bronze Age Mycenaean political and administrative apparatus between ca. 1200 and ca. 1100 B.C. In short, the palace-centered bureaucracies were vital to society because they had become the main means of maintaining record keeping, collective agriculture, and architectural and artistic skills; and when they disappeared, there was nothing to replace them. "It seems clear," writes University of Missouri scholar William R. Biers,

> that the mainland palaces represented
> the heart of the Mycenaean system,

SHIPWRECKS—TIME CAPSULES FROM PAST AGES

A good deal of the recently discovered archaeological evidence for life in Greece in the Archaic Age has come from excavated shipwrecks. In this excerpt from *The Visible Past*, noted scholar Michael Grant explains some of the ways that examining old wrecks has increased our knowledge of that remote era.

"For at least four thousand years, a large proportion of the world's goods has traveled by sea, and it is believed that until less than two centuries ago as much as five percent of all this material was lost, every year, by shipwreck. . . . During the first millennium B.C., for example, it has been estimated that as many as 15,000 merchant ships and 5,000 warships went down in the Mediterranean Sea alone—the richest museum of underwater antiquities in the world. . . . An ever-increasing number of such vessels has been located, both in shallow and in deep water, every one of which is a "time capsule" adding to our comprehension of ancient shipbuilding, trade routes, and maritime traffic in general. . . . One such historic discovery was the archaic Greek ship found [in 1961] in the waters beside the island of Giglio, the ancient Igilium, off the coast of Tuscany [in western Italy]. The vessel lay at a depth of 150 feet. . . . It proved to have sunk in about 600 B.C., during the Archaic period of Greek history. Our information about this period is patchy, but the Igilium ship has done something to rectify this, for although many objects from the vessel suffered dispersal, what remained has given us a more intimate understanding of . . . the trading ships and operations which played so large a part in its life. . . . [For example,] the pottery on board the Igilium ship came from six or seven separate geographical locations [ranging from eastern Greece to western Italy]. . . . Evidently . . . commercial patterns and networks [in the Archaic Age] were a good deal more intricate and highly developed than there was previously any reason to believe."

and when that system ceased to exist, society changed. When the palaces fell, their bureaucracy disappeared, and with them the need for and eventually the knowledge of writing. The same thing happened to large-scale architecture and representational art.[11]

Still, Greece was neither primitive nor stagnant during the Dark Age. As early as the mid- to late eleventh century B.C., new ideas and skills were filtering in from the outside. The most obvious example is the introduction of iron smelting (from the Near East, where it had long been known; probably via Cyprus, the large island lying south of Asia Minor), which spread across Greece between ca. 1050 and ca. 950. This was a major advance, since tools and weapons made of iron are tougher and keep their edges better than those made of bronze.

The early Dark Age was also a time of large population movements. The reasons for these migrations are far from clear, but

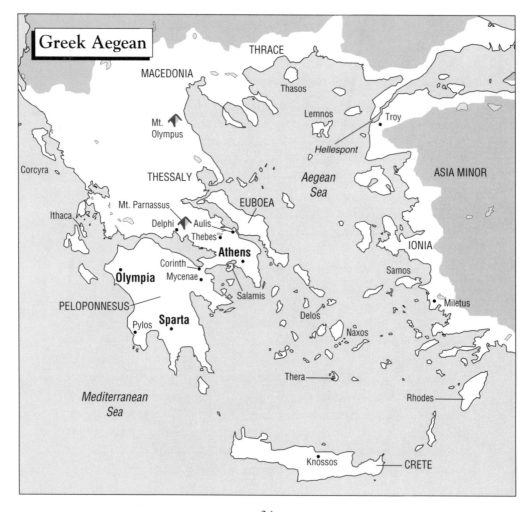

many mainland Greeks appear to have been displaced by other migrants who were *entering* Greece, including a tribal people, the Dorians, from the Balkan region south of the Danube River. Most of those who were displaced crossed the Aegean and settled on the coasts of western Asia Minor. This area, in which dozens of Greek communities eventually grew and prospered, later came to be called Ionia. Other mainlanders may have migrated in search of better farmland and other opportunities for a fresh start.

Dark Age Society and Its Leaders

Social and political life during the Dark Age was centered on individual villages (in contrast to the citylike palace-centers of Mycenaean times). The local leader was known as the *basileus*. "The Greek word *basileus*," Sarah B. Pomeroy and her colleagues write,

is usually translated as "king" wherever it appears in literature, including [Homer's] *Iliad* and *Odyssey*. It would be misleading, however, to call the Dark Age leaders "kings," a title that conjures up in the modern mind visions of monarchs with autocratic powers. A more appropriate name for the Dark Age *basileus* is the . . . term "chief," which suggests a man with far less power than a king. The *basileus*, nevertheless, was a man of great stature and importance in the community. . . . The construction and renovations of the chieftains' homes required the time and labor of a substantial number of persons, unlike the ordinary houses, which could be built by the occupants themselves. The chiefs' houses may also have had some communal functions.[12]

Archaeologists discovered the remains of a powerful Dark Age chieftain, his wife, and possibly their house in 1981 at Lefkandi, a site in the western part of Euboea (the large island lying along the eastern coast of the Greek mainland). The centerpiece of the find was a finely decorated bronze amphora (jar) containing a man's ashes. These cremated remains were wrapped in strips of cloth, some of which have survived in an excellent state of preservation. (Physical examination of the cloth, coupled with comparisons to painted depictions of cloth on vases, has greatly increased knowledge of early Greek textiles.) Beside the amphora rested an exquisite iron sword and spearhead, which surely only a well-to-do or powerful person could have afforded to own at that time. Also close beside this burial were two others—the skeleton of a woman who had been buried wearing a golden necklace and other fine jewelry, and the skeletons of four horses, probably the man's chariot team.

These magnificent burials, clearly those of socially prominent individuals, were made beneath the floor of a large houselike structure that was deliberately knocked down and covered by a mound of earth and stones directly after the funeral. The largest Dark Age building yet discovered, the structure, erected ca. 1000 B.C., measured about 146 by 30 feet and had a high roof supported by wooden pillars. Although it may have served as the chief's home and/or served some communal functions, its connection to the burials and the manner of its destruction suggest that it was also a *heroon*, a special site designed to honor or worship the memory of a hero or royal personage.

Scholarly opinion generally holds that the large size of the Lefkandi building and the unusual finery attending the burials it contained were exceptional for the early Dark Age. If so, the buried man, sometimes

An excavator hands an artifact that he has discovered in a Greek tomb to a colleague.

referred to as the "Hero of Lefkandi," may have been the leader of a small pocket of Mycenaean society that had survived the catastrophe of the previous century. Such a situation is not all that surprising; for scholars have long suspected that the Mycenaean settlement at Athens also survived the upheavals for a while, until the inhabitants slowly lost most of their heritage and began to build a new culture.[13] Archaeologists may eventually bring to light other temporary

pockets of Mycenaean survival, succeeding, as they did at Lefkandi, in making the Dark Age seem a little less dark.

It is almost certain that most of the Dark Age villages and their leaders were a good deal less splendid than those at Lefkandi. The political or governing institutions for villages and groups of villages described in Homer's epics, which scholars believe roughly reflect average examples from the late Dark Age, were fairly simple. A group of local chiefs, headed by an overall chief, met in a council (*boule*) to decide policy for the whole community or people (*demos*). To achieve a consensus in the community, the chiefs presented their ideas and decisions to an assembly of the fighting men, who gave their approval. The overall chief probably also led public sacrifices to the gods and conducted "diplomatic" relations with chiefs from neighboring regions. As portrayed in Homer's works, society was male dominated and generally characterized by a competitive spirit, the desire to be recognized as "best" (*aristos*) and thereby to acquire honor and respect (*time*). As would prevail in later ages in much of Greece, women had no political voice and for the most part obeyed the rules set by their fathers, husbands, and other male relatives.

The Transformation of Farming and Fighting

Eventually, Greek society began to grow more complex, vigorous, prosperous, bold, and creative, marking the start of one of history's most profound economic, political, and cultural transformations. First, during the late Dark Age and early Archaic Age, the population began to rise again, which helped to spur important agricultural developments. These included more intensive cultivation of olives and vines and a corresponding reduction in the prevalence of pastoralism (the raising and herding of livestock), which had been the main means of food production in Mycenaean times and the early Dark Age.

Agricultural changes promoted the spread of small independent farmers, who created a veritable revolution in agriculture, and warfare as well. Noted classical scholar Victor D. Hanson calls it "an enormous transformation . . . nothing less than the creation of an entire class, which through sheer preponderance of numbers overwhelmed" the chiefs and other traditional aristocratic rulers.[14] This class, one unlike any the world had yet seen, was made up of tough, independent men who neither needed nor wanted control by aristocratic or other ruling elites.

These self-reliant farmers became not only the economic backbone of the typical community, but also the source of its military strength. The practice of individual farmers, and later small communities of farmers, taking up arms to protect their lands, private property, and heritage against aggressors (most often other farmers) steadily led to the development of citizen militias. By the seventh century B.C., well-organized military units and tactics had developed, built around heavily armored infantry soldiers called hoplites, who wielded thrusting spears and short swords. The hoplites fought in a special formation known as a phalanx, most often composed of eight ranks, or rows, of soldiers. When standing in close order,

their uplifted shields created a formidable unbroken protective barrier. As the formation marched toward an enemy, the men in the front rank jabbed their spears at their opponents, while the hoplites in the rear ranks pushed at their comrades' backs, giving the whole unit a tremendous and lethal forward momentum. The members of local phalanxes, full-time farmers and part-time but highly effective fighters, Hanson states, "helped to establish agrarian control of the political life of their respective" communities.[15]

An Immensely Fertile Age

At the same time that these independent farmers and fighters were emerging, Greece was growing increasingly prosperous and steadily rising from its formerly backward state. Once again, scholars know this because of archaeological discoveries, especially excavations of grave sites. The sharp rise in prosperity near the end of the Dark Age "can be seen in the number of luxury goods that now turn up in graves," Biers explains.

> Imports [from foreign lands] are also found again [for the first time since the end of the Bronze Age], and

This scene, painted on a black-figure drinking cup, shows farmers plowing and sowing.

precious metals reappear. Thin bands of gold foil shaped by being hammered in stone molds appear in Athens in the ninth century [B.C.]. . . . By the second half of the eighth century [B.C.] they were being decorated with animal friezes [decorative strips containing carvings or sculptures], which are generally considered to indicate [Near] Eastern influence.[16]

Another Near Eastern import, an alphabet borrowed from the Phoenicians (a maritime trading people who inhabited the coasts of Palestine), made possible the reemergence of reading and writing in Greece. In turn, this led to the beginnings of written literature, including the commission of Homer's epics to paper (actually papyrus, a parchment made from an aquatic plant) some time in the Archaic Age.

The immensely fertile Archaic Age witnessed a veritable host of other economic and cultural developments. Accompanying the return of literacy was the expression of new, more rational (what might be termed scientific) views about the universe, as opposed to traditional supernatural conceptions. In the late seventh century B.C., Thales of Miletus (the leading city of Ionia), perhaps the world's first philosopher-scientist, theorized that everything in the natural world might be a form of one universal, underlying physical substance; and he is said to have invented geometry, based partially on Egyptian mathematical ideas. The Archaic Greeks also began to develop monumental architecture, most conspicuously in religious temples, which were at first made of wood but eventually of stone. In addition, the ongoing expansion of both

AN ARCHAIC GREEK POET SAVES HIS SKIN

Little is known about the life of one of Greece's earliest poets, Archilochus, beyond that he was born sometime in the early seventh century B.C. on the central Aegean island of Paros and took part in the colonization of the northern Aegean island of Thasos. His poems survive only in quotations by later writers and in a few papyrus fragments. They are written in a variety of meters, range in tone from deep melancholy to sparkling wittiness, and often reveal his personal feelings, even when they are less than noble. In one famous verse, for example, he freely admits that he is no hero, having tossed his shield away in the midst of battle to better facilitate his escape: "Well, what if some barbaric Thracian glories in the perfect shield I left under a bush? I was sorry to leave it—but I saved my skin. Does it matter? O hell, I'll buy a better one" (quoted in The Classical Greek Reader).

One particularly fine example of Greek monumental architecture is the Tholos in the sanctuary of Athena at Delphi. Its ruins, seen here, show that it was a circular building.

the population and foreign trade set in motion a burst of colonization. In the late 700s and early 600s B.C., settlers from various Greek cities established new towns along many of the coasts of the Mediterranean and Black Seas. Still another hallmark of the Archaic Age was the growth of Panhellenism, the concept that all Greeks were culturally united, if not politically so. This concept was exemplified by shrines, oracles, and athletic games attended by all Greeks, including the famous shrine and oracle at Delphi (in central Greece), which dispensed divine prophecies, and the Olympic Games, initiated, according to tradition, in 776 B.C.

Widespread Political Experimentation

Meanwhile, the Archaic Age was also a time of political growth and experimentation and the crucial formative period of Greek democratic institutions. The region's many isolated communities, which had developed separate, individual identities during the Dark Age, emerged as full-blown city-states in the eighth century B.C. The Greeks called the city-state the polis (plural is poleis). Most typically, each polis consisted of a town built around a central hill, or acropolis, and surrounded by small villages and farmland. But though the majority of city-states had such physical similarities and felt linked by their

ARCHAIC GREEK MARRIAGE CUSTOMS

Little is known for certain about marriage and other relations between men and women in Archaic Greece. Apparently, prior to marriage an exchange of property took place, in the form of *hedna*, or "bridewealth," gifts the groom gave the bride's father. Based on passages from Homer's works and other evidence, scholar Sue Blundell (in a passage from her book *Women in Ancient Greece*) suggests the following scenario for upper-class marriages in that era:

"The process of competing for the hand of a powerful man's daughter began with an exchange of courtship gifts (or *dora*) between the suitors and the prospective father-in-law, a ritual which served to establish friendly relations between the two parties. The suitors then put in their "bids" for the young woman by making promises of bridewealth (*hedna*) which would only be accepted once the marriage had been definitely agreed. . . . The women involved in all of these marriage arrangements seem, unsurprisingly, to have had little or no say in their own futures. Clearly, among the upper classes of Archaic Greece marriage was seen as an institution that established a relationship, not so much between a woman and a man as between a father-in-law and a son-in-law."

common language, religious beliefs, and heritage of myths from the Age of Heroes, they evolved differing local governments and traditions. This is why they came to think of themselves as tiny separate nations and were so often reluctant to unite.

A crucial part of what differentiated the polis of Archaic and later times from the simple Dark Age community was the development of increasingly sophisticated political institutions to meet the needs of a local people. In most states, power passed from the hands of chieftains to ruling councils composed of several community leaders (at first

exclusively aristocrats). This form of government is known as oligarchy, from a Greek word meaning "rule of the few." Some states, for example Corinth (in the northern Peloponnesus), retained their oligarchic councils for several centuries.

In many other Greek states, however, where the common people steadily grew disenchanted with aristocratic rule, new forms of government evolved. Beginning in the mid-600s B.C., for instance, ambitious individuals in several leading cities gained power by exploiting growing anti-aristocratic sentiments. The Greeks came to call these men, who were essentially petty dictators, "tyrants." The negative definition of the term "tyrant"—an "oppressive leader"—developed later, for a number of tyrants, at least at first, upheld most local laws, supported the arts, and enjoyed wide popular support. But as a form of government, tyranny was unstable and short-lived in Greece. This is because a tyrant needed popular support, especially from his community's soldiers, to stay in power. The citizen bodies of many city-states, which included the soldiers, increasingly came to eliminate the tyrants and to assume governing authority themselves.

This trend toward democratic ideals and government was spearheaded by Athens, which began its rise to greatness in late Archaic times. There, in 594 B.C., with the aristocrats and common people poised on the brink of civil war, the opposing factions called on a prominent citizen named Solon to arbitrate a solution. He proceeded to cancel all debts, create a new, fairer system of laws, and to increase opportunities for nonaristocrats to climb the social ladder. "To the mass of the people I gave the power they needed," Solon is reported to have remarked afterward,

> neither degrading them, nor giving them too much rein. For those who already possessed great power and wealth I saw to it that their interests were not harmed. I stood guard with a broad shield before both parties and prevented either from triumphing unjustly.[17]

Solon's social and legal reforms laid the necessary groundwork for the emergence of a full-fledged democracy, the world's first, in Athens some eight decades later. This event would prove to be part of the prelude to the Classic Age, in which Greek civilization would reach its political and cultural zenith.

CHAPTER THREE

THE CLASSIC ACHIEVEMENT: ATHENS'S CULTURAL GOLDEN AGE

Over the past few centuries, travelers to Athens have regularly stood in awe of the still majestic remains of the Parthenon and other buildings on its central hill, the Acropolis. These structures have come to symbolize the "glory that was Greece" in general, and Athens's cultural golden age in particular. Indeed, in the fifth and fourth centuries B.C., the period modern historians refer to as Greece's Classic (or Classical) Age (ca. 500–323 B.C.), Athens produced a tremendous burst of political and artistic creativity. The mid- to late fifth century was especially productive and fertile in this respect. "Never in the history of the world," comments noted historian Chester G. Starr, "have so few people done so much in the space of two or three generations. Impressive in itself, the Classic era was also a seminal influence for all later Western civilization."[18] During this short span of years, Michael Grant adds, "the Athenians excelled at tragic drama, history, philosophy, sculpture, architecture and painting. This simultaneously classic achievement in so huge a variety of fields was startling and unequalled."[19]

Athens spearheaded the Greek "classic achievement" because for almost two centuries it was the largest, most populous, wealthiest, one of the most powerful, and always the most influential of the Greek city-states. It was also the most openly and staunchly democratic. These factors—along with others of a political, economic, and cultural nature—somehow combined in just the right way at the right time to produce something rare, unique, and brilliant. Pericles (ca. 495–429 B.C.)—the great Athenian leader whose name became synonymous with the golden age (sometimes referred to as the "Age of Pericles")—sensed these special qualities. "Future ages will wonder at us," he correctly predicted, "as the present age wonders at us now."[20]

Power in the Hands of the People

A number of important events, trends, and political and cultural changes marked the transition from the Archaic Age to the Classic Age; and it is debatable which of these was most pivotal. Certainly two events stand out as particularly crucial and influential, especially in establishing the energetic and creative spirit of the new age. The first was Athens's establishment of the world's first true democracy. Solon's political reforms in the 590s B.C. had given unprecedented rights to the general nonaristocratic citizen body, the *demos*, and thereby increased the power of the middle and lower classes; and it was only a matter of time before these classes acquired complete political authority.

The turning point came about the year 508 B.C. The popular leader Cleisthenes, an aristocrat involved in a power struggle with rival aristocrats, saw the wisdom of offering the commoners more of a say in government in return for their support. And thus, as Herodotus later memorably put it, he "took the [common] people into his party."[21] In a key move, Cleisthenes and his supporters greatly increased the powers of the Assembly, a group of male citizens that had long met from time to time to discuss and debate community affairs. It now gained considerable powers, which it exercised with increasing boldness in the decades that followed. In addition to directly electing some public officials, the new Assembly had the sovereign authority to declare war, make peace, create commercial alliances, grant citizenship,

An Athenian politician addresses the people. Athens was the first nation-state in history in which a majority of power was vested in the ordinary citizenry.

found colonies, allocate public funds for construction and other projects, and decide foreign policy. The sweeping nature of these powers is best illustrated by the body's wartime responsibilities. The assembled citizens determined the overall strategy, how many soldiers or ships would be employed, and which generals would command. (The generals chosen then planned and carried out the specific battlefield strategies and tactics.) No other citizen body in human history, including those of the most liberal modern democracies, has ever wielded so much direct authority in state affairs.

The new system, with its thorough mix of people from all social classes, operated, at least in theory, on the principle of equality under the law (*isonomia*). According to Grant:

> The *isonomia* of Cleisthenes, though it did not all come into force at once, but emerged gradually, was a sophisticated, intricate, and experimental array of new political institutions, adding up to the most democratic form of government that had so far been devised by human ingenuity, and establishing the essential features of Athenian society for 200 years.[22]

This unprecedented political freedom had important consequences. It not only effected sweeping transformations of Athenian government and society, but also had the residual effect of promoting the freedom of artistic and creative expression, a key factor in the golden age to come. Athens's open democracy also inspired other Greeks; in the years that followed its inception, numerous poleis, seeing the advantages of the Athenian system, set up their own democratic governments.

Persia's King Xerxes, whose forces invaded Greece in 480 B.C., is pictured in this hypothetical early modern rendering.

The Greco-Persian Wars

Another pivotal event (actually a series of events) marking the transition to the Classic Age was the Greek response to invasions launched by the Near Eastern realm of Persia. The largest empire the world had seen up to that time, Persia then controlled most of what are now Iran, Iraq, and Turkey, including the Greek cities of Ionia (which it had first subdued in the late sixth century B.C.). In 490 B.C. the Persian king, Darius I, sent a large army to vanquish Athens.[23] At Marathon, on the seacoast about twenty-five miles northeast of the city, a smaller force of Athenian hoplites met and soundly defeated the invaders, who retreated back into Asia.

Seeking revenge for this affront, the next Persian king, Darius's son Xerxes (ZERK-seez), returned in 480 with over 200,000 troops and a thousand ships, the largest invasion force ever assembled in ancient times. Persia's goal was now nothing less than the conquest of all of Greece, a foothold from which it might later launch expeditions into other parts of Europe. As the huge Persian host approached Athens, the inhabitants fled to nearby islands; and on or about September 17, Xerxes led his troops into the deserted city. He ordered them to destroy the existing temples and other buildings atop the

AN EYEWITNESS DESCRIBES THE BATTLE OF SALAMIS

In his play the *Persians*, first produced in 472 B.C., the Athenian playwright Aeschylus, who fought in the sea battle at Salamis, describes how Greek sailors and hoplites, after gaining the advantage, slaughtered the terrified enemy by the thousands. In this excerpt (from Philip Vellacott's translation), a messenger tells the Persian queen mother:

"Then from the Hellene [Greek] ships rose like a song of joy the piercing battle-cry, and from the island crags echoed an answering shout. The Persians knew their error; fear gripped every man. They were no fugitives who sang that terrifying paean [battle hymn], but Hellenes charging with courageous hearts to battle. . . . At once ship into ship battered its brazen beak. A Hellene ship charged first, and chopped off the whole stern of a Persian galley. Then charge followed charge on every side. At first by its huge impetus our fleet withstood them. But soon, in that narrow space, our ships were jammed in hundreds; none could help another. They rammed each other with their prows of bronze; and some were stripped of every oar. Meanwhile the enemy came round us in a ring and charged. Our vessels heeled over; the sea was hidden, carpeted with wrecks and dead men; all the shores and reefs were full of dead. Then every ship we had broke rank and rowed for life. The Hellenes seized fragments of wrecks and broken oars and hacked and stabbed at our men swimming in the sea. . . . The whole sea was one din of shrieks and dying groans, till night and darkness hid the scene. . . . Never before in one day died so vast a company of men."

Acropolis, confident that he was dealing Athens a blow from which it could never recover.

But Persia's so-called "great king" was dead wrong. The embers of the fires that had swept the Acropolis were still glowing when the Greeks, fighting for their homes and way of life, initiated a desperate and valiant counteroffensive. On September 20, 480 B.C., three days after his army had entered Athens, King Xerxes mounted a hill overlooking the narrow Salamis Strait, a few miles southwest of the city. There, he watched in horror as a Greek fleet made up of warships from many city-states delivered his much larger naval forces a crushing defeat. The Greeks followed up this win with others the following year, including the almost total annihilation of the Persian land army at Plataea, north of Athens. The Greek victory was so complete and decisive that no other Persian army ever entered Europe again.

Moreover, in a twist no one could have predicted, Greece's darkest hour proved to be an important stimulus to its subsequent development of cultural grandeur. The victory

An eighteenth-century woodcut depicts the large sea battle fought between the Greeks and Persians at Salamis in September 480 B.C. The Greeks won a stunning victory.

instilled in the Greeks a feeling of immense accomplishment. They had demonstrated to the world—and also to themselves—that they, like their ancestors at Troy, were capable of glorious deeds. And the defeat of the world's greatest empire seemed only the first step toward other, equally noteworthy achievements. In this way, historian W. G. Hardy remarks, the victory over Persia became "the torch to set fire to the brilliance of the great age of the Greeks. There was a tremendous upswelling of confidence . . . [and now] the Greeks felt that there was nothing they could not attempt."[24]

As the wealthiest and most populous Greek city-state, Athens felt and demonstrated this new confidence more than any of its neighbors. With amazing energy and boldness in the decades following the great patriotic war, the Athenians generated a prodigious flurry of political, economic, and cultural creativity. Athens had emerged from the conflict as one of the two most powerful and prestigious Greek cities (the other being Sparta, in southern Greece); and it quickly exploited that power and prestige by taking the lead in the establishment of the Delian League, a confederation of over a hundred city-states intended to guard against further Persian incursions. In the decades that followed, the audacious and increasingly aggressive Athenians transformed the alliance into their own lucrative maritime empire. And the considerable moneys generated ended up funding the ambitious and expensive building programs that became one of the chief hallmarks of Athens's golden age.

A Visual Expression of the Athenian Spirit

The highlight of these programs was the creation of a majestic complex of temples and other structures atop Athens's Acropolis to replace those destroyed by the Persians. The new works owed their inspiration and political backing largely to Pericles, a leader of extraordinary intelligence, vision, and imagination, as well as keen political skills. What better way to demonstrate that Athens was the marvel of Greece, he asked his countrymen, than by celebrating and honoring the city's patron deity, Athena (goddess of wisdom and war), whose divine favor had been instrumental in Athens's rise to greatness? Building new, grand, and beautiful temples to her would ensure her continued protection, he proposed. At the same time, a new and magnificent Acropolis complex would be the ultimate symbol of Athenian imperial greatness. Indeed, as Plutarch would later write, this ambitious project was seen, both at the time and by posterity, as Pericles' and Athens's greatest achievement:

> There was one measure above all which at once gave the greatest pleasure to the Athenians, adorned their city and created amazement among the rest of mankind, and which is today the sole testimony that the tales of the ancient power and glory of Greece are no mere fables. By this I mean his construction of temples and public buildings.[25]

Thousands of Athenians, free and slave, citizen and noncitizen, worked side by side on these projects, which required a wide variety of skills to complete. The most comprehensive description of the various kinds of workers involved is that from Plutarch's biography of Pericles, listing those who toiled to raise the Parthenon:

ARCHAEOLOGICAL STUDY AND PRESERVATION OF THE PARTHENON

The Parthenon, the most architecturally perfect and perhaps the most famous building ever erected, survived the ages in an excellent state of preservation until 1687. In that year a cache of gunpowder stored inside by the Turks, who then ruled Greece, exploded, severely damaging the temple. Subsequently, it rapidly fell into an advanced state of ruin.

Serious archaeological examination and restoration of the Parthenon could not begin until the Turks relinquished control of Greece, which finally occurred in the 1830s when Greece gained its independence. Almost immediately, archaeologists began clearing the Acropolis of modern structures and fortifications and collecting and cataloguing broken fragments of its ruined temples. Between 1842 and 1845, Greek archaeologist Kyriakos Pittakis made the first major attempt to restore parts of the Parthenon. Other restoration projects were mounted in 1872 by Greek architect Panayis Kalkos and in 1899–1902 and 1922–1933 by Greek scholar Nikolaos Balanos.

By the late 1960s and early 1970s, scientific studies of the Parthenon and the other Acropolis monuments showed that acid rain and other environmental factors were causing them to deteriorate with alarming speed. Such concerns led the Greek government to form the Committee for the Preservation of the Acropolis Monuments in 1975. Headed by Greek architect Manolis Korres, the committee—made up of architects, archaeologists, civil engineers, and chemists—compiled a detailed study and comprehensive restoration plan. The restoration began in the 1980s and is not expected to reach completion until sometime in the early twenty-first century. The committee's goal is not to restore the Parthenon to its fifth-century B.C. condition. Rather, the intention is to halt its decay, give it structural stability, and preserve it as a noble ruin so that future generations can behold and be inspired by this wondrous achievement of a long-vanished people.

A restoration of the Parthenon in its original glory.

The small temple of Athena Nike (sometimes referred to as the Wingless Victory) stands atop its stone platform on the right wing of the Propylaea, on the western side of the Acropolis.

The materials to be used were stone, bronze, ivory, gold, ebony, and cypress-wood, while the arts or trades which wrought or fashioned them were those of carpenter, modeler, coppersmith, stone-mason, dyer, worker in gold and ivory, painter, embroiderer, and engraver, and besides these the carriers and suppliers of the materials, such as merchants, sailors, and pilots for the sea-borne traffic, and wagon-makers, trainers of draft-animals, and drivers for everything that came by land. There were also rope-makers, weavers, leatherworkers, road-builders, and miners. Each individual craft, like a general with an army under his separate command, had its own corps of unskilled laborers at its disposal . . . [and consequently] the city's prosperity was extended far and wide and shared among every age and condition in Athens.[26]

As posterity has shown, the workers' labors produced nothing less than spectacular results. When most of the complex reached completion near the end of the fifth

This reconstruction of the Parthenon's eastern pediment rests in Athens's Acropolis Museum. Zeus (seated on his throne) has just given birth to Athena (with spear and shield).

century B.C., a grand stone staircase led up the western side of the hill. Perched on a stone platform on one side of the stairway was the tiny Temple of Athena Nike, graceful and elegant in its own right but providing a mere foretaste of the wonders beyond. At the top of the staircase loomed the Propylaea, a massive and magnificent column-lined entranceway leading onto the summit. Beyond this portal sprawled the heart of the complex—a mass of temples, outdoor shrines and altars, walkways of polished marble, and magnificent bronze and stone statues.

Dominating the entire summit of the Acropolis, of course, was the breathtaking sight of the Parthenon. Designed by the architect Ictinus and master sculptor Phidias (a close friend of Pericles'), it was 237 feet

long, 110 feet wide, some 65 feet high, and incorporated over 22,000 tons of exquisite marble (mostly quarried at Mount Pentelicon, about ten miles northeast of Athens's urban center). Inside stood Phidias's splendid thirty-eight-foot-high statue of Athena, with garments fashioned of beaten gold. Simultaneously simple and ornate, and seemingly possessing both serene reserve and bursting energy, the Parthenon was a visual expression of Athens's special spirit. The structure is "clear reasoning," Greek scholar John Miliadis remarks,

> and yet filled with humanity; it is not directed to the mind so much as to the eye and the soul; it means to move the spirit and to ennoble it. It is more like a living organism than a

mechanical creation. It is more the work of inspiration than calculation. It is a new vision of life, the vision of classical Athenians.[27]

Sculpture and Painting

The Parthenon and other imposing classical temples were lavishly adorned with beautiful sculptures and/or paintings; and numerous freestanding statues and wall paintings appeared not only in Athens, but all over Greece in the Classic Age. Not surprisingly, their creation kept busy a small army of talented painters and sculptors.

One of the most gifted of the classical Greek painters was Polygnotus (flourished ca. 475–447 B.C.), who was born on the northern Aegean island of Thasos and painted mostly wall murals. One of his stylistic innovations was to spread his figures across the painting, rather than in a single line, the most common method of earlier painters. "He imposed the figures on a neutral, dark background after preparing them in his workshop, then somehow attaching these to the wall surface," scholar George D. Wilcoxon explains.

His method of indicating depth was simply to place some figures above the others. His coloring is said to have been light and even without much variety. But above all, he was renowned for the boldness and vividness of his forms, their clear, concise outlining, the alive faces and open mouths suggestive of human emotion. . . . By a general agreement too, his figures were "ideal," "better than ourselves,"

[demonstrating] in his medium what the greatest sculptors and architects did in theirs—that nobility of character and idea which is the inner spirit of Classicism.[28]

Polygnotus's most famous painting, which unfortunately has not survived, was the *Capture of Troy*, displayed at Delphi. Luckily, we have an idea of what it looked like, for the later traveler Pausanias described it in his guidebook, saying in part:

As you go into the building [the so-called "club-house," which long housed some of Polygnotus's finest works] on the right is the painting that shows the fall of Troy and the Greeks sailing away. Menelaus's men are getting ready for the voyage [back to Greece]; there is a painting of the ship with a mixture of men and boys among the sailors, and the ship's steersman Phrontis standing amidships holding two poles. . . . [Some men] are taking down Menelaus's tent not far from the ship. . . . Briseis is standing with Diomedes above her and Iphis in front of them as if they are all gazing at Helen's beauty. Helen herself is standing with Eurybates near her. . . . Above Helen sits a man wrapped in a purple cloak, extremely melancholy; you would know it was Priam's son Helenos even before you read the inscription.[29]

Some of Polygnotus's other murals were displayed at Athens, as were many of the finest Greek statues and other sculptures. The temples usually had statues, life-size or larger, in their pediments (the triangular gables at

To create such a statue, the sculptor often set up a temporary workshop near the site it would occupy, so as to minimize the risk of damage when moving the finished work. The first step was to make a clay model, often full-size, supported by a wooden or metal frame. Guided by the master sculptor, apprentices completed the model based on his design, and after he had given his approval, they roughed in the broad proportions in the marble version. He finally took over, providing the details and finishing touches. The master would work "quite swiftly," says art historian John Boardman,

> with the sharp iron point that brought off large marble flakes. Then the . . . claw chisel, which safely gouged broad swathes on the stone, then the flat chisel, and rasps and rubbers to smooth away the tool marks. Where dress fell in deep, shallow-catching folds, or there was deep cutting to be attempted between the legs of horses . . . then the bow drill was brought out. An assistant spun the shaft, and rows of close-set holes were drilled straight into the surface to define masses which could be safely broken away, leaving the chisel to finish the folds of drapery, or intricacies of anatomy.[30]

This superb sculpture of a horse, in the Acropolis Museum, dates from just after 500 B.C.

front and back), and sculpted reliefs in their friezes (ornamental bands running around the perimeter just above the colonnade). Other buildings besides temples featured decorative sculptures; and many large freestanding statues—of gods, military heroes, winning athletes, and so on—adorned various parts of Athens as well as other Greek cities.

After the sculptors finished carving such figures, other craftsmen took over. Where needed, metalworkers attached precast bronze spears, horse harnesses, and other details to holes the sculptors had drilled in the appropriate places. Then painters applied wax and bright colors, bringing the statues to life. They used the wax to polish the surfaces representing flesh, producing the look of sun-tanned skin, then painted the hair, lips, and eyebrows a deep red, and the clothes and other trappings various shades of red, blue, and yellow. (The painters also applied liberal coats of bright colors, especially reds and blues, to various outer sections of temples and other large structures. Over many centuries these colors faded and wore away, leaving the stark off-white stone façades familiar today.)

The Potter's Art

A more refined mode of painting was integral to the production of pottery, long one of Greece's chief industries. Using hands-on techniques inherited from artisans of prior centuries, the master potters of the Classic Age molded wet clay (*ceramos*) on wheels and fired it in kilns reaching a temperature of 1,000 degrees Fahrenheit. They crafted their wares for practical use, to be sure. Yet they strove for originality of design and excellence

An impressive early example (ca. 515 B.C.) of the red-figure pottery style. The vessel, a calyx krater, used for mixing wine and water, is attributed to the painter Euphronios.

43

of execution in every piece. According to Thomas Craven, an authority on ancient art, their wares

> were part and parcel of the routine life of the people. Vases were designed to hold flowers and fruits, or as decanters for wine, or as storage jars. Beautiful cups were fashioned for drinking purposes and all sorts of table china were decorated with religious scenes. The ceremonials in the temples and at . . . altars necessitated a great variety of sacred vessels; the holy olive oil given as a prize in the Panathenaic games required a container of impeccable artistry, as did those of other festivities such as a special form of amphora, with a long neck, which held the water for the bridal bath—and was also used as a monument for those who died unmarried. The exquisitely shaped *lekythus*, a bell-mouthed, narrow-necked, single-handed vase, was filled with fragrant oils and buried with the dead or left at the graveside.[31]

In the century preceding the Classic Age, most such vases, amphora, and other vessels utilized the "black-figure" decorative style pioneered by Athenian artisans, including Sophilos, the first potter known to have signed his work. In this style, figures of men were painted in black on the natural buff-colored background of a fired pot. The artist then used a pointed tool to etch details into the figures. Black-figure pottery reached its height of popularity between 550 and 525 B.C. in the work of an unnamed artisan whom scholars refer to as the "Amasis Painter."

Not long afterward, a new style, the "red-figure," appeared. In a reversal of the older style, red-figure technique left the figures of humans and animals in the fired pot's natural reddish tone and rendered the backgrounds black. This allowed for the application of more realistic details, which were applied with a brush (although etching was still employed for certain fine details). Red-figure pottery was perfected in the early 400s B.C. by such Athenian artisans as the so-called "Berlin Painter," who excelled at portraying human limbs and muscles.[32]

The Invention of the Theater

The theater was another visual art that flowered in classical Athens. In fact, this unique combination of art form and public entertainment, which millions of people in many lands have enjoyed over the centuries, originated in Athens in the sixth century B.C. Its subsequent development was rapid and spectacular. In less than a century, a series of informal songs and speeches recited by worshipers in roadside religious processions evolved into formal dramatic competitions held in large public facilities. Almost all of the theatrical concepts familiar today—including tragedy, comedy, acting, directing, costumes, scenery, and even theater tickets and acting awards—were invented in Athens shortly before and during the Classic Age.

The dramatic competitions were part of the City Dionysia, a religious festival held in March in honor of the fertility god Dionysus. The festival opened with a splendid procession of thousands of people, who marched through the city to its theater. The first Athenian theater was erected perhaps in the early 530s B.C. Its exact location and physical layout are unknown. But evidence suggests that it was in the Agora (marketplace) and that it consisted of a circular "dancing place," or orchestra, where the actors performed, and an audience area (*theatron*) with wooden bleachers. About 499 B.C. these bleachers collapsed in the middle of a performance, killing many of the spectators.

After this unfortunate incident, the Athenians constructed the Theater of Dionysus against the southeastern base of the Acropolis. In its initial form, the theater featured an orchestra eighty-five feet in diameter. To avoid another disaster, the seating, which could accommodate up to fourteen thousand spectators, consisted of wooden planking covering earthen tiers carved into the hillside. (In a fourth-century B.C. renovation, the wooden seats were replaced by stone versions.) A rectangular structure called the *skene*, or "scene building," was erected behind the orchestra and facing the audience. The *skene* provided a background for the actors and also housed dressing rooms and perhaps a storage area for stage props.

THE THEMES OF GREEK TRAGEDY

In this excerpt from his edition of Aeschylus's only surviving trilogy, the *Oresteia* (published as *The Orestes Plays of Aeschylus*), noted translator Paul Roche summarizes the major themes of fifth-century B.C. Greek tragedy.

"[They came] principally from the old stories of the gods and heroes as handed down by oral and written tradition in epic and lyric poetry, particularly from the *Iliad* and *Odyssey* of Homer. Homer became a kind of bible-*cum*-history of the ancient world, and a compendium of its values. Occasionally a drama was built upon contemporary history, as in *The Persians* of Aeschylus. . . . [Theater] never quite lost its religious motive and impetus . . . [and maintained] a powerful moral and ethical sense which sought not only to inspire but to teach. . . . Man's ways with . . . the gods— and vice-versa—are explored . . . side by side with the ever-important and always bewildering questions of destiny, freedom, personal responsibility, and sin. . . . [Also presented are] man's ways with man: honor, justice, retribution, law, liberty, duty; and his universal emotions: love, hate, revenge, fear, pride, pity, and regret. These are the themes and emotions that pulse through the stories taken by [Athenian playwrights] . . . and turned into dramas of surpassing power, significance, and beauty."

After the City Dionysia's great procession reached the theater, a bull was sacrificed to Dionysus and the contests began. Over the course of a few days, several playwrights presented their works, which at first were exclusively tragedies. The three masters of Greek tragedy were Aeschylus (ca. 525–456 B.C.), Sophocles (ca. 496–406 B.C.), and Euripides (ca. 485–406 B.C.). Their stories came mostly from mythology and explored the relationship between humans and gods, as well as basic human emotions and social and moral themes of interest to all. When comedy was introduced in the early fifth century B.C., it provided audiences with an emotional release and relief from the grimness of the tragic presentations. The comic plays also became an important outlet for political expression by poking fun, often with unheard-of candor, at institutions, leaders, and other citizens. No one accomplished this better than the comic master Aristophanes (ca. 445–385 B.C.).

Admission to the theater was free at first; but increasing demand for seats soon necessitated the introduction of tickets (about 450 B.C. by Pericles). By the mid-fourth century, a seat for the day cost two obols (about one-quarter of an average worker's daily wage). Archaeologists have uncovered a number of these tokens, which look similar to coins and are made of bronze, lead, ivory, bone, or terra-cotta (baked clay).

The Theater of Dionysus, seen from the southern rampart of the Acropolis. The seating originally consisted of wooden benches; the stone versions were added in a later renovation.

Having watched all of the plays, the spectators remained seated to witness the festival's most eagerly anticipated moment—the awards ceremony. A panal of ten judges issued lists that rated the work of participants in four categories—tragic playwrights, comic playwrights, leading tragic actors, and leading comic actors. The winner in each category received a crown of ivy similar to those awarded to Olympic victors.

Like the theater, all of the art forms, along with the political form of democracy, invented in Greece and perfected there in the Classic Age remain with us today. Some, such as tragic drama and monumental architecture, were rediscovered during the European Renaissance and helped to shape the subsequent development of European culture. As William Biers puts it, this "emphasizes and reflects the essential unity of Western civilization and the debt that we today owe to those people in a small land far away and long ago."[33]

CHAPTER FOUR

GREEK SOCIETY: SOCIAL GROUPS, CITIZENSHIP, AND POLITICAL INSTITUTIONS

Because each Greek city-state was in a sense a separate nation, it developed its own local social and political customs. So the nature of the people who made up society, their social groups and status, concepts of citizenship, and the way they governed themselves varied from one Greek city or region to another. Still, certain basic social groups and concepts—for instance the family, the tribe, male political dominance, the institution of slavery, and so forth—were more or less the same everywhere.

Unfortunately, scholars remain unsure about the nature and degree of the differences and similarities among individual Greek societies, which could also vary from one historical period to another. This is because almost all of the surviving evidence for Greek social and political institutions comes from Athens, and mostly from the Classic Age. It may be safe to say that many of the more basic Athenian social institutions and customs described below were similar to those in the majority of Greek states. However, the society of Athens's archenemy, Sparta—about which

scholars know a fair amount—was radically different in a number of ways. Even if Spartan life was extreme and atypical for Greece, a brief review of certain aspects of Spartan society shows the considerable diversity of ancient Greek social settings.

Family and Social Identity

Despite such diversity, some social units or groups were common to all Greeks, the smallest and most basic being the family, or *oikos* (the plural is *oikoi*). It usually included not only the members of the "nuclear" family familiar in modern American society (parents and children), but also grandparents and other relatives; all property, including land and slaves; and the tombs of ancestors. The *oikos* was "the basis of one's security and social identity," says scholar N. R. E. Fisher, "and the main source of one's social and religious obligations and relationships."[34]

The first such obligation was to make sure that the family did not die out. Since Greek society was patriarchal (dominated by men), family leadership and property ownership usually passed from father to son; so it was essential for the head of the family to produce a son, or if necessary to adopt one. In classical Athens, the law "appears to have allowed a man without a son to adopt someone, normally an adult, into his *oikos*," Fisher explains,

who then left his former *oikos* and resigned any claims to any part of it; the "father" would thus attempt to ensure both the continuation of his line and also that maintenance in old

age and performance of correct burial rites which a father who had brought up children could socially and legally demand from them in return.[35]

When the head of the household had more than one son, the sons eventually established their own *oikoi*, which remained linked to the parent family through strong kinship ties. This was the basis of the next largest social group, the clan, or *genos* (the plural is *gene*). The average clan consisted of a group of families that claimed descent

The splendor depicted in this early modern reconstruction of the marketplace at Sparta is highly exaggerated. Archaeological evidence suggests that its appearance was far more modest.

from a common ancestor. In the affairs of the extended family, the heads of the *gene* were usually more influential than the heads of individual households. It was common, for example, for a clan leader to arrange marriages for his various sons, daughters, nephews, nieces, cousins, and grandchildren, who might come from many different *oikoi*.

Larger Social Units

The next units in the widening social pyramid were the phratry and the tribe, both highly extended kinship groups. In Athens the typical phratry, or "blood brotherhood," consisted of about thirty clans, comprising about as many people as lived in an average Greek village. Often the focus of social gatherings and religious rituals, a phratry was similar to a modern religious congregation, except that the members of a phratry were related to one another. The exceptions to this rule were people who, because of various circumstances, had no family or clans. Phratries sometimes adopted, or welcomed into their ranks, such unfortunate individuals.

This relief, carved for a person's tomb sometime between the first and third centuries A.D., shows a family banquet. Scenes of family life appeared often in tombs.

INSCRIPTIONS REVEAL INFORMATION ABOUT SOCIAL HISTORY

Although some of the limited information available about ancient Greek people and their social status and customs comes from surviving literature, the written sources portray only part of the picture. To help fill in some of the gaps, scholars rely on archaeological evidence, including vase paintings showing scenes from everyday life, and especially inscriptions carved into wood, metal, and, most often, stone. Among the many different kinds of inscriptions are tombstone epitaphs, religious dedications, both public and personal announcements of various kinds, administrative and commercial lists, law codes, political decrees, and even graffiti. In contrast to most formal written sources, inscriptions, particularly those from tombs, often provide bits and pieces of personal information, opinions, and occasionally even feelings and emotions. These can make ancient Greek society seem less distant and more tangible. "One of the principle features of the study of Greek inscriptions," remarks scholar A. G. Woodhead in his book on Greek inscriptions, "is the closeness of contact which they give us with the ancient world."

The tribe, or *phyle* (plural is *phylai*), the largest single social unit, commonly consisted of three phratries. Each Greek city-state had its own traditional tribes, the numbers of which varied from state to state and are unknown for most states. Athens long had four traditional tribes, until about 508 B.C. when Cleisthenes introduced some important social reforms as part of his democratic revolution. According to Herodotus, he

changed the number of Athenian tribes from four to ten, and abolished the old names. . . . He named the new tribes after other [mythical] heroes, all native Athenians . . . appointing ten [tribal] presidents—*phylarchs*—instead of the original four.[36]

Cleisthenes' reforms also divided the Athenian territory of Attica into approximately 140 small geographical units, or community districts, called demes. These became the focus of many of the social and religious activities of the phratries and new tribes. The demes and new tribes were arranged in such a way that each tribe contained people from each of Attica's three general regions—the urban area, the coastal areas, and the inland areas.

One reason for this new arrangement was to ensure a more reliable military force. Before, each tribe had provided an unspecified number of soldiers for the army (which was a part-time militia rather than a standing army), and on a more or less voluntary basis. Under the new plan, each of the ten tribes

51

was required to supply a minimum number of troops during a military emergency. This meant that the army would be both larger and drawn more evenly and fairly from all quarters of society. At the same time, the reformers hoped to reduce the influence of the traditional phratries and tribes, which had too often feuded among themselves and/or placed their own local interests above those of the polis. Under the new system, Fisher explains, "each man found himself grouped with others from all over Attica, and thus it was hoped that local loyalties, which had been strong and disruptive during the sixth century, might be diminished."[37]

Citizens Versus Noncitizens

A Greek's social identity was determined not only by the family and other social groups to which he or she belonged, but also by his or her status as an individual. One was either free or unfree (i.e., a slave), for example, and either a citizen of the polis or a noncitizen; and these distinctions were extremely important, for free people and citizens had more rights and privileges than slaves and noncitizens. Specific rules regarding status and citizenship varied from polis to polis, but it is likely that something fairly close to the Athenian system prevailed in most other states.

Although classical Athens had an extraordinarily open democracy that accorded citizens a great deal of freedom, it defined the term "citizen" rather narrowly by modern standards. Only free males born in Attica were *politai*, meaning "citizens with political rights." These included the rights to take part in meetings of the Assembly, hold public office, sue someone in court, and sit on a jury.

By contrast, free men who lived and worked in Athens but who were born outside of Athenian territory (either Greeks from other city-states or non-Greeks) were not citizens. Known as metics (*metoikoi*), they were mostly merchants and tradespeople, such as potters, metalsmiths, and jewelers. By modern standards, the fact that they could neither take part in government nor own land seems unfair, for they made important contributions to the community, including providing essential goods and services, paying taxes, and serving in the army when needed. Like Athens, other Greek states denied resident foreigners citizenship and full civic rights. At Sparta and some other poleis, for example, they were called *perioikoi*, or "dwellers round about," because they were expected to live in their own villages or neighborhoods, apart from the citizenry. (The term *perioikoi* was also applied to some people born in Spartan territory who were denied citizenship for one reason or another.)

For a Greek, then, full citizenship, with all of its rights and advantages, was much coveted and cherished; and its loss, known as *atimia* (literally, "dishonor"), was highly dreaded. In Athens, stripping someone of citizenship was the stiffest penalty delivered by the courts short of exile or death. An *atimos*, a man whose citizenship had been revoked, could not speak in the Assembly or law courts, hold public office, or enter a temple or the marketplace. And the community as a whole strictly enforced these sanctions; for example, any citizen who saw an *atimos* in a prohibited area was allowed to arrest him on the spot.

The Status and Rights of Women

Although native-born freemen were certainly the most privileged group in any Greek state, they were not the only ones who held citizen status. Their female rela-

A nineteenth-century illustration reconstructs a street in ancient Athens. The structure at left, the Tower of the Winds, built about A.D. 40, has survived in an excellent state of preservation.

tives were considered citizens too, but a special type. In Athens they were called *astai* (meaning "members of the community"). An *aste* had no political rights; however, she did have the civic rights to take part in and/or benefit from the community's religious and economic institutions. Thus, for example, citizen women played roles, often important ones, in various religious festivals.

Still, for the most part, women in classical Athens led restricted, protected lives.

They could not appear in court and, with rare exceptions, they could not own land. Moreover, most Athenian women spent a majority of their time in the home, forbidden to venture out into the streets except when accompanied by a male relative or household slave. Legally speaking, women were under the control of their guardians, who were always men. When a woman's husband was still living, he was her guardian in all legal matters. If he died and her sons

It is important to emphasize that not all Greek poleis legally restricted women to this degree. In Sparta, for instance, the laws regulating women's rights and behavior were considerably more liberal. Spartan women were not largely confined in the home and, more significantly, were allowed to own their own land. Although Spartan inheritance laws remain unclear, apparently a daughter could inherit a share of her father's land even when she had brothers, her share being half that of a male. And if she had no natural or adopted brother, she likely inherited the family property directly, without the obligation of marrying a male relative, as an Athenian woman in such a situation was expected to do. As a result, a good deal of land eventually fell into the hands of Spartan women. The famous Athenian philosopher-scholar Aristotle, who complained in his *Politics* that female Spartans had entirely too much freedom, reported that in his day (the mid-fourth century B.C.) they owned fully two-fifths of the land in Sparta. And Plutarch mentions a number of wealthy Spartan women, including the mother of King Agesilaus, who "took a prominent part in public life, and with so many dependents, friends, and debtors was a figure of great influence."[38]

An Athenian grave stele, dating from about 340 B.C., *shows a man named Kephisokritos with his daughter, Stratyllis. A father remained a woman's guardian until she married.*

were not yet of age (legal adulthood for Athenian males began at age eighteen), her guardianship reverted to her father, who had been her guardian before her marriage. In the case of a widow with young sons, once they came of age she could choose either to remain under her father's guardianship or to become the ward of one of her sons. A woman's guardian, whoever he may have been, was obligated to support her financially and also to protect her, both physically and legally (in legal contracts, court cases, and so on).

Similar female property-owning privileges prevailed at Gortyn, a Greek city-state in southern Crete. We are fortunate to have a series of inscriptions from Gortyn that constitute the most complete surviving Greek law code. The code shows that, as in the case of women in Sparta, women in Gortyn inherited land, livestock, and/or money from their fathers' estates even when they had brothers (although their shares were smaller than their brothers'). Moreover, Gortynian women retained control of their property as divorcées or widows.

These facts about the relatively enlightened customs and laws pertaining to women in Sparta and Gortyn do not begin to tell the whole story of the status of women in these states, of course. As was true elsewhere in Greece in the Archaic and Classic Ages, Spartan and Gortynian women had no political rights and therefore no say in government. And ultimately they were seen as the weaker gender and therefore naturally subordinate to men. Still, comparing these customs and laws with those in Athens clearly illustrates how widely the treatment and opportunities of women varied from place to place in ancient Greece at any given time.

Slaves—Their Exploitation and Treatment

All of the members of a Greek community mentioned so far had some kind of civic rights, even if they were not citizens. This was not the case, however, with another important segment of the population—slaves, who enjoyed neither citizenship nor civic rights. Legally speaking, slaves were simply a form of property. They were, in a sense, human machines because they performed a large proportion of the physical labor in all social areas and occupations in every Greek community.

In classical Sparta, most menial labor was done by helots. Though not slaves in the strict sense (agricultural serfs being a more accurate description), they constituted nothing less than an enslaved social class.[39] Like slaves, they had no rights and were closely regulated. They were also, on the whole, treated more cruelly and inhumanely than slaves in other Greek city-states. For example, it was a common and accepted rite of passage for a young Spartan military trainee to stalk and kill one or more helots before becoming a hoplite.

Such large-scale exploitation and inhumane treatment of slaves and helots was possible because the Greeks, like other ancient peoples, automatically accepted the institution of slavery as ordained by the gods and a part of the natural way of things. Even great thinkers like Aristotle and his equally famous mentor, the philosopher Plato, who envisioned utopian (ideal) societies in their writings (Plato's *Republic*, for example), could not imagine a society operating efficiently without slave labor. And the slaves themselves probably thought no differently, for the few slaves who managed to earn their freedom immediately acquired slaves of their own.

Greek slaves were typically captured in wars or bought from slave traders. Because Greeks usually frowned on enslaving other Greeks, most slaves in Greece were "barbarians," the prevailing term for

An undated engraving, probably from the eighteenth century, depicts the Greek biographer Plutarch.

SOME PEOPLE SLAVES BY NATURE?

This is an excerpt from the section of Aristotle's *Politics* (quoted in Thomas Weidemann's *Greek and Roman Slavery*) in which he defines the slave and argues that slavery is part of nature's design.

"A human being who by nature does not belong to himself but to another person—such a one is by nature a slave. A human being belongs to another when he is a piece of property as well as being human. A piece of property is a tool which is used to assist some activity, and which has a separate existence of its own. . . . All men who differ from one another by as much as the soul differs from the body or man from a wild beast . . . these people are slaves by nature, and it is better for them to be subject to this kind of control. . . . For a man who is able to belong to another person is by nature a slave (for that is why he belongs to someone else). . . . Nature must therefore have intended to make the bodies of free men and of slaves different also; slaves' bodies strong for the services they have to do, those of free men upright and not much use for that kind of work, but instead useful for community [i.e., political] life. . . . Of course the opposite often happens—slaves can have the bodies of free men, free men only the souls and not the bodies of free men. After all, it is clear that if they were born with bodies as admirable as the statues of the gods, everyone would say that those who were inferior would deserve to be the slaves of these men. . . . To conclude: it is clear that there are certain people who are free and certain who are slaves by nature, and it is both to their advantage, and just, for them to be slaves."

non-Greeks. They came mostly from Asia Minor or from Thrace and other regions lying north of the Aegean Sea. A family of moderate means probably kept two or three slaves; a well-to-do household might have fifteen to twenty; and shops and other commercial enterprises would have even more. An Athenian metic named Cephalus, for example, used about 120 slaves in his prosperous shield-making business. The Athenian state also owned slaves, which it used in its silver mines at Laureum, in southern Attica. Mine slaves were shackled day and night, worked in horrendous conditions, and had no hope of gaining freedom.

Household slaves, by contrast, were generally well treated and often became trusted members of the family. Although some owners no doubt hit or flogged such slaves, the law usually prevented severe brutality. And a free person who beat or killed another person's slave could be prosecuted. Household slaves also frequently received small wages that they could either spend or save up to buy their freedom; or freedom might be granted by a kind master as a reward for long years of trusted service. Athenian freed slaves (freedmen) had the same social status as metics, which meant that they had no political rights. But also like metics, they were free to become as successful as they desired. And a few did; when he died in 370 B.C., for instance, a freedman named Paison was the richest manufacturer in Athens and left behind a valuable estate.

Such success stories remained exceptional, however, for the vast majority of Athenian and other Greek slaves never gained their freedom. The lucky ones were those who, through circumstances they could not control, found more or less comfortable niches in the homes of kind or at least fair-minded masters.

Varying Political Institutions

Each Greek city-state, therefore, was made up of various kinship groups (family, clan, phratry, and tribe) and also several social groups and classes of varying legal status and rights (male citizens, female citizens, noncitizen resident foreigners, and slaves). There were also some similarities among the political institutions of most Greek states. By the Classic Age, for example, most had an assembly in which male citizens met to choose certain leaders and to discuss and/or vote on state policy. Most also had a council, a smaller ruling body of advisers, elders, or legislators who proposed new laws. And all had public magistrates (administrators or rulers) to run the government and carry out the laws and state policy. However, the nature, interactions, and degree of authority of these three kinds of political entities could vary considerably from one state to another. A brief examination of the governments of Corinth, Sparta, and Athens in the Classic Age illustrates the range of variation.

After several decades of rule by tyrants (dictators), in late Archaic times Corinth became an oligarchy and remained so for the next two centuries. The exact way the government operated is uncertain. But it appears that the authority of the assembly, made up of middle-class farmer-hoplites, as was the case in other Greek poleis, was contained or overshadowed by that of two relatively small groups of rulers. These were the council, composed of some eighty legislator-elders, and a handful of powerful magistrates, the *probouloi*.

The political situation in classical Sparta was more complex and controversial. Described by Aristotle as a mixed system of monarchy, oligarchy, and democracy, Sparta's government was considered unusual by most other Greeks. By this period, the vast majority of Greek states had long since gotten rid of their kings (or chieftains) and instituted oligarchies or democracies. However, Sparta retained its kings (two ruling jointly at all times), although their powers were overshadowed in all but religious and military matters by other elite political groups. These included a council (the *gerousia*) of thirty elders; an assembly (the *apella*), composed of freeborn Spartan males (the Spartiates); and five very powerful magistrates, the ephors ("overseers"). Scholars continue to debate the relative powers of these groups within the Spartan government. But it is probably safe to say that the ephors—who were elected annually by the assembly and held far-reaching administrative and judicial authority—significantly limited the powers of the assembly, council, and kings.

By contrast, in those Greek states that instituted democracy, most governmental authority was vested in the local assemblies,

This modern drawing depicts Athens as it may have looked in the second century A.D., when it was part of the Roman Empire. By that time, Greek cities were no longer autonomous.

and the decisions and directives made by an assembly were carried out by the local council and magistrates. In classical Athens, for instance, the Council (*Boule*), made up of five hundred legislators chosen by lot (random selection), drew up recommendations, in effect legislative bills dealing with state business and the community in general. The members of the Assembly then debated and voted on these bills. If a majority voted for a bill, it became a decree with the force of law. The Assembly could also change a bill by adding amendments or by sending it back to the Council to be reframed; or the voters could reject the bill outright. The Council also made sure that the decisions made by the Assembly were duly carried out by overseeing the financial and other administrative business of the community. This task was accomplished by various Council subcommittees (boards of councillors), which closely supervised the magistrates. The magistrates, who actually ran state affairs on a daily basis, included nine administrators (the archons) and ten generals (the *strategoi*), elected annually by the Assembly.

Ostracism and Archaeology

Another way that democracies differed from monarchies and oligarchies in Greece was that the democracies instituted various safeguards designed to maintain and protect the rule of the people. Perhaps the best known such safeguard was the system of ostracism, possibly introduced at Athens by Cleisthenes and subsequently adopted by a number of other Greek states.[40] University of British Columbia scholar Malcolm F. McGregor here explains the Athenian version of the procedure, meant to prevent one leader from amassing too much power:

Each year the Athenians voted . . . whether to hold an ostracism. In the event of an affirmative vote, the citizens, a few weeks later but before elections . . . reassembled. Each one scratched on a shard [a piece of broken pottery called an *ostrakon*] the name of the man who seemed most to threaten [political] stability; such, at any rate, is the theory [because the exact procedure is still uncertain]. He who polled the most votes (6,000 had to be cast) withdrew from the polis for ten years without loss of property or citizenship.[41]

Modern scholars know about ostracism and the names of some of those ostracized and banished partly from accounts in surviving literary texts (some of Plutarch's biographies, for example). But archaeological discoveries have been particularly helpful in illuminating this and other related aspects of Greek political and social history. According to William Biers:

The excavations in the Athenian . . . marketplace, and in the [nearby] Kerameikos Cemetery . . . have uncovered some thousands of *ostraka* bearing the names of participants in various votes that were held throughout the fifth century [B.C.]. In ancient Greece a citizen's full name consisted of his given name plus that of his father and/or the place where he lived. Here, then, are original historical documents written by the hands of ordinary citizens. They not only provide

59

evidence of a political process, but also yield information on the spelling, pronunciation, grammar, and styles of composition used by the fifth-century Athenians. The appearance of names of people well known from the works of ancient authors and of some previously unknown, together with the excavation evidence and even the types of pottery used as *ostraka* add to our knowledge of the social and political history of Athens.[42]

CHAPTER FIVE

GREEK SOCIETY: EVERYDAY LIFE, CUSTOMS, AND BELIEFS

In most ways, everyday life in an ancient Greek community was as varied, complex, and rich as it is in the United States and other modern societies. And most of the basic social institutions, customs, and pastimes common today had their Greek counterparts. As people still do today, for instance, the Greeks farmed the land; lived in houses with bedrooms, kitchens, and bathrooms; went shopping; got married and divorced; educated their children; threw parties; took part in religious worship; conducted business and trade; worked out at the local gym; and staged athletic contests, both on the local and national level.

Still, if it was possible for an average modern person to go back in time and visit a Greek polis in the Classic Age, he or she would likely find the experience strange and disconcerting. Because there were no telephones, radios, televisions, and so on, communication was strictly by direct word of mouth and letter. And transportation was interminably slow by modern standards; people mostly walked from place to place, or else utilized mules, horses, and sailing ships. So it routinely took days, weeks, and even months for news, correspondence, trade goods, and people to circulate throughout the Greek world.

The modern visitor to ancient Greece would no doubt also find certain Greek attitudes, beliefs, practices, and other aspects of daily life odd, extreme, or in some cases disturbing. For example, the Greeks were far more concerned with maintaining family lineage and also family honor than most people are today. Greek women were second-class citizens; marriages were arranged by relatives; children routinely received corporal punishment; and slavery, now seen as unjust and inhumane, was an accepted feature of everyday life. Although there were doctors, they did not know that disease is caused by germs and lacked most other medical knowledge and devices taken for granted today; so life expectancy was far lower than it is today, and the incidence of death from illness or during childbirth far higher. Moreover, the average Greek polis was a small and extremely tight-knit community in which most people knew one another, there were few secrets, and tradition and conformity were encouraged. Finally, religion played a more prominent role in Greek life than it does in modern society. Religious worship permeated almost every aspect of community life, from the home to athletic games; for it was believed that an unappeased or angry god might vent its wrath on the whole community.

Farmers and Crops

Still another thing that would immediately strike the modern visitor to ancient Greece would be the sudden dividing line between the city and the country. Unlike most modern cities and towns, which thin out gradually, with suburbs forming buffers between urban and rural areas, Greek cities ended abruptly, often at imposing defensive city walls. So when people left the crowded city, they passed immediately into the quiet countryside, where the only human habitations were small villages and farms.

Farms and farmers were, in a very real sense, the lifeblood of a Greek community. First, throughout Greece's history, land remained the principal basis of personal wealth, and local economies and a majority of Greeks made their living by growing crops or raising livestock. Also, the capital (wealth) produced by Greek farms made city life and its amenities possible. On the one hand, the commodities produced by farmers generated and maintained marketplaces, around which cities grew and thrived. Also, some wealthy landowners moved to the city, relying on hired managers (bailiffs) to look after their estates, and pursued or supported politics, trade, or artistic and intellectual endeavors. In these ways, Victor Hanson states, farming "created the surplus and capital to allow a significant minority of the population to shift its attention from farming and to pursue commerce, trade, craftsmanship, and intellectual development." In addition, a community's more numerous small farmers made up the bulk of its local political assembly and military militia. "Only a settled countryside of numerous small farmers," says Hanson, "could provide the prerequisite [required] mass for constitutional government."[43]

The staple crops these farmers produced were cereal grains (especially barley and wheat), lentils, olives, grapes, figs, and other fruits and vegetables. And the most common animals raised were sheep and goats, although pigs, horses, and other sorts of livestock were important in certain areas. For example, Thessaly, in central Greece,

A stele, dated to about 400 B.C., shows an Athenian woman, Hegeso, holding her jewelry box.

A group of terracotta figurines, from the early–sixth century B.C., captures a farmer using his oxen to plow his field. Plowing and sowing were usually done in October.

was known for its horses. Although most city-states in the Classic Age were more or less self-sufficient in these staple crops, some of the larger ones had to import certain essentials. An often-noted example is that of Athens, which imported well over half of its grain from the fertile fields of Greek cities lying along the coasts of the Black Sea.

As a rule, the farmers of mainland Greece and its nearby islands sowed their grain in October, in order to take advantage of the short winter rainy season. (Spring and summer in much of the region are long, hot, and arid.) One person steered a wooden (sometimes metal-tipped) plow, pulled by oxen or mules, while a companion followed along tossing the seeds. Harvest time was in April or May. Farmers left their fields fallow (unplanted) for the rest of the spring and summer to enable the soil to replenish itself; meanwhile, the harvested grain was threshed (separated from the stalks) by having mules trample it on a stone floor.

The planting calendar was different for other crops. Grapes, for example, were usually picked in September. Some of these were saved for eating, but most were crushed to make wine. By contrast, farmers harvested olives between October and January and either picked them by hand or used sticks to knock them out of the trees. The Greeks ate some of the olives and used the rest to make olive oil, which they used in cooking, making beauty products, and as a fuel for oil lamps.

Typical Greek Houses

Modern scholars know relatively little about the physical appearance of the homes in which farmers dwelled, or for that matter about Greek houses in general. This is because surviving written sources provide no detailed descriptions and the meager remains of only a few such structures have been excavated. All too often in attempting to reconstruct ancient houses, says noted classicist Ian Jenkins, the archaeologist is faced with scanty or uncertain evidence. Usually nothing survives above ground and perhaps only the indication of where a building once stood is a murky outline staining the earth. Scattered debris may indicate how the walls were constructed and the roof covered. Anything that could be salvaged from the house, however, is likely to have been

---

OIL LAMPS HELP ARCHAEOLOGISTS TO DATE THEIR FINDS

In this excerpt from his informative book *The Archaeology of Greece*, noted scholar William R. Biers tells how excavators sometimes date ancient Greek archaeological finds by noting the style of the oil lamps (if any) found on the site.

"A common find in the strata [layers of earth] of the Greek period are fragments of terra cotta lamps. The production of oil lamps began in the seventh century [B.C.] and ran without interruption throughout antiquity in classical [Greek and Roman] lands. As common archaeological finds they are a great help in chronology, for their types changed with some regularity [and excavators know with some certainty the period in which each style flourished]. They have therefore been more intensively studied than other classes of minor objects. . . . The earliest seventh-century [B.C.] lamp was a simple shallow saucer with the rim pinched out at one point to form a nozzle, providing a place for a wick. . . . [These] lamps actually had no rims as such, but late in the century the side walls were curved over to form a flat rim and the nozzle was elongated. . . . The typical Athenian oil lamp of the sixth century [B.C.] is a further development of the types current in the last century. Made on a wheel . . . such a lamp invariably has an oval nozzle added to the body at a point where a section of the rim is broken away. . . . Lamps continued to develop. . . . A common variety of the first half of the [fifth] century [B.C.] . . . has a raised band around the filling hole, forming a rim."

removed in antiquity. Stone foundations, for example, are liable to have been robbed and used elsewhere.[44]

Sometimes, however, archaeologists make a lucky find. In the late 1960s, for example, the fairly well-preserved remains of a country farmhouse dating from the fourth century B.C. were discovered in Attica. Its original form was simple—a rectangle about fifty-eight by forty-five feet, with its four sides laid out around a central courtyard open to the elements. There were porticoes (roofed porches) on some sides, and one corner of the structure was raised to form a two-story

tower, a defensive position to where the farmer and his family probably retreated in times of danger.

Evidence suggests that most Greek townhouses, including those of well-to-do families, were also simple in design and built around a central courtyard. Commenting on some twentieth-century excavations of several one- and two-story houses near Athens's marketplace, John Pedley writes:

> Generally they are small with a single entrance from the street into a courtyard surrounded by several rooms . . . . The courtyard provided light and air,

One of many archaeological sites in Attica, the large territory controlled by ancient Athens. In the late 1960s, the remains of a country farmhouse were discovered there.

since windows on the exterior were few and far between for reasons of security. . . . Normally one chief room opened off the court, and this was used for entertaining. It was called the *andron* and it was here that men dined reclining on couches. . . . A kitchen, identifiable by quantities of crockery and cooking utensils, was nearby. There was also a bathroom/latrine, a small room with a drain which emptied into a drain outside the house. Other rooms around the court were storerooms, living rooms (those frequented by women [and] identified from quantities of loom-weights), or bedrooms, though these were often on the second floor.[45]

The construction materials and furnishings of such houses were also fairly basic and unimpressive. Typically, each featured a stone foundation and walls made of sundried clay bricks. Although the bricks were sometimes reinforced with wooden timbers, the walls were not very strong or durable; and the bricks began to crumble after a few years, forcing home owners to undertake frequent repairs. In poorer homes, the floors might consist of earth beaten hard and covered with straw mats, layers of pebbles, or perhaps flagstones. Those who could afford it used mosaic tiles and rugs imported from Asia Minor. Roofs were most often made of baked pottery tiles. Most, if not all, Greek houses also had a small altar at which the family members prayed; a hearth and some braziers (metal containers that burned charcoal) to supply heat; and near the front door a *herm*, a bust of the god Hermes (patron of travelers), resting on a pedestal about three or four feet high. (It was thought that his likeness kept evil from entering the house.)

Women's Household Duties and Authority

Whatever the location, size, layout, and furnishings of a Greek dwelling, the household within almost always operated under the authority and rules of the father or eldest male in the family, referred to as the master. Yet he rarely actually ran the household. This was because most Greek men busied themselves with farmwork, business, politics, or leisure pursuits and spent only a minimal amount of time in the home. So a man's wife (or his mother, daughter, or sister in some cases) customarily managed the household on a daily basis. Her duties usually included cleaning, cooking, spinning, weaving, making the clothes, managing the slaves (if any), and paying the bills with money allotted by the master.

The degree of freedom men allowed women within the home depended on where in Greece the family lived. In Athens and presumably a number of other states in the Classic Age, the women of the family had the run of the house most of the time; but not so when the master was entertaining male guests who were not part of the extended family or clan. Because it was considered unseemly for the women to be seen by, let alone to mix with, nonfamilial men, the ladies of the house retired to the *gynaeceum*, the "women's quarters." Depending on the size of the house, this consisted of one or more rooms, located in the back of single-story houses and upstairs in those with two stories, in which they engaged in spinning, weaving, and visiting with female guests. The Roman writer Cornelius Nepos, who visited Athens not long after the Classic

Age, found such segregation of women odd and compared it unfavorably to the custom in his own society:

> Many actions are seemly according to our [i.e., the Roman] code which the Greeks look upon as shameful. For instance, what Roman would blush to take his wife to a dinner-party? What matron does not frequent the front rooms of her dwelling and show herself in public? But it is very different in [Athens]; for there a woman is not admitted to a dinner-party, unless relatives only are present, and she keeps to the more retired part of the house called "the women's apartment," to which no man has access who is not near of kin.[46]

In classical Sparta, by contrast, women were not nearly so regulated and segregated. In fact, it appears that Spartan women did not simply manage the household for their husbands, as Athenian women did, but actually set the rules and largely took precedence over men in that sphere. This was because Spartan society (beginning in the Archaic Age) was built around a strict, regimented system (the *agoge*) designed to produce machinelike soldiers to man the most feared army in Greece. Spartan boys left home at age seven and up to the age of thirty or more lived in military barracks with other males. In fact, Spartan men were not allowed to reside with their wives and children until age thirty. And even then, married men were frequently absent, engaging in military training, war,

This nineteenth-century woodcut depicts a group of well-to-do Greek women engaging in routine household duties while a domestic slave does some laundry nearby.

hunting, and political activities; in addition, most Spartan men of all ages ate their meals with their comrades in a common mess hall. "One result of this system," says scholar Sue Blundell,

> was that the authority of the individual father was downgraded. . . . There can be little doubt that one effect of undermining the father's role would have been to enhance that of the mother, who by the time her husband moved into the family home would have established her pre-eminence there. . . . [The] radical separation of the public and private spheres . . . would have ensured that female domestic power was accepted and possibly even officially encouraged.[47]

Love, Marriage, and Divorce

It is reasonable to ask how women in Athens and other states that closely regulated and segregated them were able to meet eligible men, fall in love, and decide to get married. The answer is that this familiar courting process is a relatively modern one. As a rule, Athenian and most other Greek marriages were arranged by fathers or clan leaders, and it was not unusual for a young bride and groom barely to know each other before their wedding night. Marriage was not a women's decision, therefore, and social customs surrounding marriage did not encourage or even take into consideration the notion of falling in love. Some evidence suggests that romantic love did exist; but probably few couples were fortunate enough to experience it.

On the whole, marriage was most often a legal arrangement made by men—the prospec-

A painting on a fifth-century B.C. *red-figure* pyxis *(toilet box) shows a wedding scene.*

tive bride's father or other male guardian and the prospective husband. In the Classic Age the deal was made at a formal betrothal, usually in front of witnesses. Along with the woman, valuable assets changed hands in the form of her dowry (money her father provided for her maintenance). After the marriage arrangement was sealed, plans for the wedding celebration began. No complete descriptions of the ceremony itself have survived. However, Blundell provides this credible scenario, pieced together from various literary and visual sources:

> The public part of the ceremony began with a wedding feast in the house of the bride's father. At nightfall, the partially veiled bride, the groom and the groom's best friend were carried to the couple's future home in a nuptial

chariot drawn by mules, accompanied by a torchlit procession of friends and relatives singing nuptial hymns. . . . At their destination the bride was greeted by her mother-in-law, who was carrying torches, and was formally conducted to the hearth, the focal point of her new home. Meanwhile, bride and groom were showered with nuts and dried fruits, emblems of fertility and prosperity, and a boy crowned with a wreath of thorns and acorns circulated among the guests distributing bread from a basket. . . . The climax of the proceedings came when the bride was led by the groom towards the bridal chamber, while a wedding hymn was sung by the guests. . . . On the following day . . . gifts were presented to the couple by the bride's father and other relatives.[48]

If an Athenian marriage did not work out, divorce was usually an easily obtainable option. When a man initiated the divorce, he simply sent his wife from the house, usually to live with her male relatives. (Customarily he retained custody of the children.) A woman who wanted a divorce had to acquire the aid of a male relative (or some other male citizen), who on her behalf brought the case before an archon.

The marriage process was markedly different in Sparta than it was in Athens. In his *Life of Lycurgus*, Plutarch tells how Spartan girls paraded nude in processions and also competed in athletic games in full view of young men, who thereby began to form attractions for them. Here, he describes the strange nocturnal ritual that a Spartan bride and groom enacted in the early months of their marriage:

The custom was to capture women for marriage. . . . The so-called "bridesmaid" took charge of the captured girl. She first shaved her head to the scalp, then dressed her in a man's cloak and sandals, and laid her down alone on a mattress in the dark. The bridegroom . . . first had dinner in the messes [i.e., with his male comrades], then would slip in, undo her belt, lift her and carry her to the bed. After spending only a short time with her, he would depart discreetly so as to sleep wherever he usually did along with the other young men. And this continued to be his practice thereafter. . . . He would warily visit his bride in secret . . . apprehensive in case someone in the house might notice him. His bride at the same time devised schemes and helped to plan how they might meet each other unobserved at suitable moments. It was not just for a short period that young men would do this, but for long enough that some might even have children before they saw their own wives in daylight.[49]

Childhood and Education

The ideal outcome of marriage, of course, was to produce children to perpetuate the *oikos*. Greek child-rearing customs reflected a general view of children that most people today would deem misguided and counter to the development of healthy self-esteem. In general, childhood was not viewed as an enviable, happy time of life, as it often is today, and adults felt little or no nostalgia for their youth. This was partly because they believed that children lacked proper reasoning powers,

A mother named Archestrate closely supervises her child on this fourth-century B.C. grave stele.

courage, or even a moral capacity until they were at least in their teens. And so, it was thought, young children needed to be closely watched, carefully trained, and, when necessary, harshly disciplined by parents, tutors, and other community members.

As they grew, most Greek children played with toys familiar to modern children, such as balls, hoops, tops, dolls (made of wood, clay, or rags) and dollhouses (complete with furniture), yo-yos, and miniature carts and chariots. But the most important pursuit of childhood (for males at least) was education. Young girls were trained at home by their mothers in weaving and other household arts, although some vase paintings suggest that at

least a few girls learned to read. In classical Athens, boys aged seven began attending private schools in which they learned reading and writing and eventually the verses of Homer and other poets. Boys also learned singing, playing the lyre (harp), and physical education (athletic events and dancing).

By the late fifth century B.C., higher education in Athens could be obtained for a fee from roving teachers called Sophists; they raised the ire of traditionalists, who disapproved of their use of rhetoric (the art of persuasive speaking) to make both sides in an argument seem equally valid. Beginning in the century that followed, a few young men also studied at more formal university-like schools, such as Plato's Academy (where Aristotle studied under Plato).

On the whole, education in many other Greek poleis was presumably similar to that in Athens (although conclusive evidence for most is lacking). The major exception appears to have been Sparta. There, the education of boys and young men was, like most other social institutions, built around the needs and aims of the rigid *agoge*. First, Spartan elders examined all male infants, and those considered too weak were exposed (left outside to die). Those who made it past this initial test faced years of difficult, relentless learning and training, which was subsidized and supervised by the state rather than privately run. Here, the emphasis was not on reading, writing, and other literary skills, but on the ability to endure hardships and become a strong, fearsome soldier. (There was some instruction in dancing, patriotic songs, and poetry, but these subjects took a decided backseat to military training.)

Spartan girls also received an education at state expense, the only women in all of Greece known to have enjoyed this privilege. The nature of this learning is unclear but seems to have emphasized physical fitness (probably to help facilitate having many baby boys to replenish the army ranks); some girls may also have learned reading and other skills.

Religious Worship

Like marriage, child-rearing, and education, religious belief and worship was one of the most essential aspects of Greek life. Some kind of religious ritual accompanied nearly every gathering, function, or important endeavor, both private and public. No pious Greek consumed a meal, for example, without offering a portion of the food to the gods;

religious ritual attended important life-cycle events such as birth, marriage, and death; a military general performed a sacrifice before a battle; and most public meetings, such as those of the Athenian Assembly, began with an animal sacrifice and prayers.

In contrast to the situation in most modern societies, in which religion is viewed as a private affair, the Greeks saw it as a public concern. They thought it essential to a community's welfare to maintain the goodwill of the gods. And the crime of impiety, lacking faith in or respect for the gods, was a serious one; for if one person offended the gods, it might bring down their wrath on the whole community. Moreover, most Greeks made a

An exquisite red-figure painting on the bottom of this cup, found in the Athenian territory of Attica, shows a group of young men engaging in athletic training.

71

VIEWS OF THE AFTERLIFE

Although most Greeks believed in the existence of a soul (*psyche*), their views of its possible survival in an afterlife varied considerably, as is the case in most modern societies. They expressed differing beliefs, writes University of Virginia scholar Jon D. Mikalson (in *Athenian Popular Religion*), "on such fundamental questions as whether the soul continued to exist [after death], where the souls of the dead resided, whether the souls had perception of the life of the living, and whether the souls encountered rewards and punishments in the afterlife." The most common traditional folk beliefs held that both good and bad souls descended into the underworld (Hades), guided by the god Hermes, in his manifestation as "Escorter of Souls." There, wrongdoers suffered various punishments in a ghastly place called Tartaros; while more virtuous people, particularly renowned heroes, lived on in Elysium or the Isles of the Blessed, fabled abodes of eternal happiness. However, though such beliefs still existed in the Classic Age, it is uncertain how widely they were accepted. Evidence shows that a number of classical Greeks thought, variously, that the soul lived on inside a dead person's grave marker; that it floated into the sky and lived on in moist air; or as Plato reported, that "on the very day of death it may perish and come to an end—immediately on its release from the body . . . vanishing away into nothingness" (from *Phaedo*, translated by Benjamin Jowett).

This famous sculpture of Hermes, by Praxiteles, stands in Olympia's Archaeological Museum.

connection between religion and patriotism in their belief that certain gods favored certain cities above other cities. Each city had its personal patron deity, therefore, who, it was thought, watched over and protected that community. (Athena was the patron of Athens, for instance; Hera that of Argos; and Poseidon that of Corinth.)

Such divine favoritism was not seen as coming for free, of course. Rather, the gods expected something in return. The most common view was that they would provide a certain minimum level of good fortune, prosperity, and safety as long as the people upheld their oaths (made in the gods' names); made the proper sacrifices; and consulted the gods directly when unsure about crucial religious matters, through oracles (priestesses who acted as mediums between gods and humans).

The gods that the Greeks worshiped were anthropomorphic, meaning that they were envisioned as having human form and attributes. The major gods were known as the "Olympians" because early traditions claimed they dwelled atop Mount Olympus (in northern Thessaly), the tallest mountain in Greece. These included Zeus (leader of the gods), Hera (his wife), Poseidon (god of the seas and earthquakes), Apollo (god of light, healing, and the arts), Aphrodite (goddess of love), and many others. Worship of these gods consisted of public and private prayers and sacrifices (involving various animals, plants, and liquids). The public ceremonies were often part of polis-wide religious festivals, sometimes lasting several days. The nature of these ceremonies varied from one city or region to another, partly because the Greeks had no universally recognized moral creed or sacred text (like the Bible). Still, the fact that Greeks everywhere worshiped the same pan-

This bronze statue of Zeus, leader of the gods, once held a thunderbolt in its right hand.

theon (group of gods) in roughly the same way became a unifying factor, a reminder that all Greeks shared a similar culture.

Greek Athletics and the Rediscovery of Olympia

Another such unifying factor for the Greeks was athletic training and competition. In the Archaic Age, a significant physical culture (social institutions and customs surrounding physical fitness and athletic training) developed across Greece. And by the Classic Age, the gymnasium, in which men received both physical and academic training, had became a common feature of most Greek city-states.

The importance most Greeks placed on athletics is revealed by the fact that they did not view them simply as a leisure pastime; rather, training for and competing in public games was a serious matter. This was partly because athletic contests originated as and remained always a part of formal religious worship. In events that included running, jumping, throwing the javelin and discus,

The remains of the palaestra, *a training area used mainly by wrestlers, at Olympia. The structure was originally an open courtyard surrounded by roofed walkways.*

wrestling, boxing, and horse and chariot racing, the participants dedicated their creative or physical skills and prowess to a god or gods.

In time, hundreds of local sacred games were held across the Greek world. But by the end of the sixth century B.C., four of these had emerged as preeminent. They were not only the most prestigious such events, but also international (Panhellenic, or "all-Greek") rather than local in character, drawing competitors and spectators from city-states far and wide. The greatest of all, of course, was the Olympic festival (honoring Zeus), held at Olympia (in the western Peloponnesus) every four years. The others included the Pythian Games (honoring Apollo), held at the sacred shrine at Delphi; the Isthmian Games (honoring Poseidon); and the Nemean Games (honoring Zeus).

For prizes, the victors at these games received crowns of laurel leaves or other vegeta-

tion. But there were financial rewards too, for many athletes were subsidized by well-to-do patrons; and winning athletes always received awards when they returned to their home cities. These typically included valuable bronze tripods, ornamental cups, and large jars of olive oil, which the athletes could sell for a profit. And often that was only the beginning. Like many other communities, Athens provided its Olympic winners free meals for life; and the most successful athletes were glorified almost as gods, as poets composed songs and sculptors molded statues in their honor.

For a long time, modern scholars had to be content only to read about the renowned ancient Olympics and its proud victors, for the site of the games had long before disappeared. Eventually, though, archaeologists discovered and excavated it, providing valuable information about Olympia, Greek athletics, and

Greek art and architecture as well. "German excavators . . . began work [on the site] in the 1870s," explains scholar David Gill.

> This cult center dedicated to Zeus . . . had as its focus a huge colonnaded [column-lined] temple measuring 28 by 64 meters (92 by 210 feet) which from the fifth century B.C. contained [the great sculptor] Phidias's monumental statue of the god. Digging through a layer of silt left by medieval flooding, the team discovered the substructure of the temple complete, its columns toppled by earthquakes. Amid the debris lay the pedimental sculptures described by [the ancient traveler] Pausanias [that featured] vivid depictions of the mythological foundation of the Olympic Games. . . . Relief sculptures in the metopes [rectangular panels running along the temple's sides] depicted the labors of Heracles. Further excavations have since revealed the temple of Hera, the consort of Zeus, the treasuries for individual Greek states, and the classical Olympic stadium—a linear running track one *stadion* (192.28 meters or 630 feet) long, set between parallel earthen banks that provided seating for spectators. The long tradition of excavating at Olympia has brought more recent finds too. Pausanias mentions the workshop in which the huge gold and ivory statue of Zeus was created by . . . Phidias. . . . Excavations have discovered both the workshop and debris that includes a mug with the supposedly ancient inscription "I belong to Phidias."[50]

CHAPTER SIX

INCESSANT RIVALRY AND DISUNITY: THE ANCIENT GREEKS IN DECLINE

Despite having achieved tremendous power and influence, as well as cultural greatness, the classical Greeks, like all ancient peoples, eventually went into decline and became weak enough for others to supersede them. Their decline was long, incredibly eventful, and truly tragic. It was long and eventful because it began late in the Classic Age and went on for more than three centuries. During these years the Greeks fought many wars, conquered a mighty empire, established numerous cities and kingdoms, and all the while continued to create fine art, architecture, and literature. On the surface it may have seemed that autonomous Greek cities and kingdoms, along with Greek culture, would dominate the Mediterranean sphere forever. Only in retrospect is it apparent that beneath the surface, the underpinnings of Greece's greatness and independence were rotting and crumbling.

What made this decline so tragic was the fact that its chief cause was entirely avoidable. The Greeks might indeed have continued to march at the very forefront of Western civilization for many more centuries, had it not been for their incessant rivalry and ultimate failure to unite. If the Greek city-states and kingdoms had learned to put aside their differences, to exploit their many cultural ties, and to come together into one strong nation, it is doubtful that any other empire or people in the known world could have successfully challenged them. But no such Greek unification or nation ever materialized; and the eventual result was Greece's downfall.

Modern historians have long speculated about why the Greeks so stubbornly failed to unite. Some have suggested that Greece's geography played a major role. Because it is riddled by rugged mountains and numerous islands, physically it is naturally divided into many small regions; and according to this view, the localized nature of these regions promoted the growth of not only small city-states, but also a fierce spirit of independence. Other scholars point to the Greeks' intense devotion to competition. "The Greeks were one of the most competitive peoples in history," writes historian Robert J. Littman.

Everything was made into a contest, from athletics to the great drama festivals. . . . Competition was formalized in the great *agones*, public festivals at which competitors contended. . . . Much of the competition, however, was non-productive. . . . The Greeks regarded any kind of defeat as disgraceful, regardless of circumstances. . . . Egoism, the need to excel, to gain honor and glory at the expense of others, helped to produce a society incapable of unity. The individual would not risk sacrificing himself for the city-state, nor the city-state for the welfare of Greece.[51]

Whatever kept the Greeks from forming a strong, centralized nation, their continued disunity led them to fight among themselves almost constantly. The single most damaging of these conflicts was the disastrous Peloponnesian War, fought from 431 to 404 B.C., which engulfed and exhausted most of the Greek world. Seen through the backward-looking lens of history, this watershed event can be seen as the beginning of the decline of Greek power and independence in the Mediterranean. In the two turbulent centuries that followed it, the dominance of city-states in Greek affairs gave way to that of large monarchies. And having failed to learn the lesson of unity,

The main exercise area in ancient Sparta is reconstructed in this modern drawing. Sparta's soldiers, who were long the best in Greece, underwent intensive physical training.

In one of the most famous incidents of the Peloponnesian War, an Athenian army attempting to conquer the Greek city of Syracuse (in Sicily) goes down to defeat.

these states, too, quarreled among themselves, leaving the Greek sphere open to outside aggression.

The Desire for Dominance

The Peloponnesian War was not a sudden or isolated event. Rivalry and warfare among the city-states, which had been going on for centuries, began to increase in intensity in the mid-fifth century B.C., shortly after the close of the Persian Wars. The two Greek states that had led the resistance and largely engineered the victories against the Persians—Athens and Sparta—emerged from the conflict wielding great power and prestige. Athens had Greece's strongest navy; while

Sparta possessed its most formidable land army. In the wake of the victory over Persia, each of these two states became convinced that it alone should enjoy supremacy in Greece. And when Athens engineered the creation of the Delian League and swiftly turned it into a maritime empire, Sparta responded by forming its own bloc of allies (the Peloponnesian League) and continually attempting to contain Athenian political ambitions.

By the late 430s B.C., after several decades of mutual distrust and small-scale fighting, each side finally reached a point where it was willing to wage a major war to gain overall supremacy. "The preparations of both the combatants were in every department in the last state of perfection," wrote Thucydides, who chronicled the war,

> and [I] could see the rest of the Hellenic [Greek] race taking sides in the quarrel; those who delayed doing so at once having it in contemplation. Indeed, this was the greatest movement [event] yet known in history. . . . If both sides nourished the boldest hopes and put forth their utmost strength for the war, this was only natural. Zeal is always at its height at the commencement of an undertaking; and on this particular occasion the Peloponnesus and Athens were both full of young men whose inexperience made them eager to take up arms, while the rest of Greece stood straining with excitement at the conflict of its leading cities.[52]

The so-called "great war" ended up dragging on for twenty-seven grueling years and ultimately proved ruinous for all involved. Athens went down to defeat in 404, ending its golden age, in which it had refined its democracy, raised the immortal Parthenon, and enjoyed the hegemony (dominance) of much of Greece.

The Spartan and Theban Hegemonies

The great war had caused widespread death and destruction, to be sure. But a far worse consequence was that those who had waged it had failed to learn from it the lesson that continued disunity and rivalry were futile and dangerous. The result was that the fourth century B.C. proved to be a period of further war-weariness and also political decline for the Greek city-states. At first, because it had defeated Athens, Sparta dominated Greek affairs. But the Spartans failed to maintain their hegemony of Greece, partly because they were not able administrators, and also because they were insensitive and heavy-handed in their dealings with other states. Athens responded to what most Greeks viewed as overt Spartan aggressions by building up another bloc of its own allies. And soon the two sides were at each other's throats again.

It was not Athens, however, that ended the Spartan hegemony. In the 370s B.C., a brilliant military innovator named Epaminondas rose to prominence in Thebes (located some thirty miles northwest of Athens). Under his guidance, the Thebans overhauled their military and surprised everyone by crushing Sparta's army at Leuctra (west of Thebes) in 371. Soon afterward, Epaminondas invaded the Peloponnesus, where the political climate now changed drastically. Supported by Thebes, most of the Peloponnesian cities, which had long followed Sparta out of fear, threw out their Spartan-backed regimes and instituted new governments (usually some form of democracy).

But Thebes did not retain its leading place in Greek affairs for long. Less than a decade after gaining it, the Thebans fought a major battle at Mantinea (in the central Peloponnesus), against an unlikely and decidedly temporary coalition led by Athens and Sparta. Epaminondas was killed; Theban influence rapidly waned; and afterward, according to Xenophon, who himself fought at Mantinea, "there was even more uncertainty and confusion in Greece . . . than there had been previously."[53]

THE SPARTANS FINALLY DEFEATED

The fateful battle in which Thebes, led by Epaminondas, ended Sparta's hegemony of Greece took place in July 371 B.C. near Leuctra, a village ten miles southwest of Thebes. According to the first-century B.C. Greek historian Diodorus Siculus (from his *Library of History*):

"When the trumpets on both sides sounded the charge and the armies simultaneously with the first onset raised the battle cry . . . they met in hand-to-hand combat, [and] at first both fought ardently and the battle was evenly poised; shortly, however, as Epaminondas's men began to derive advantage from . . . the denseness of their lines, many Peloponnesians began to fall. For they were unable to endure the weight of the courageous fighting of the élite corps [the Sacred Band, a unit containing Thebes's best-trained troops]. . . . The Spartans were with great difficulty forced back; at first, as they gave ground they would not break their formation, but finally, as many fell and the commander who would have rallied them [Sparta's king Cleombrotus] had died, the army turned and fled in utter rout."

Epaminondas's battle plan had succeeded with brutal efficiency. A thousand Spartans, including their king, had been slain; while the Thebans had lost just forty-seven men. In this single stroke, Thebes forever dispelled the myth of Spartan invincibility.

The Rise of Macedonia

Decades of bickering, war, destruction, and shifting political alliances had left the major mainland city-states exhausted, weakened, and vulnerable to outside attack. This time, however, the threat did not come from Asia, as it had in the previous century, but from Macedonia, a kingdom in extreme northern Greece. Its tribes had themselves long been disunited and militarily weak. The city-state Greeks had generally viewed them contemptuously as backwoods types living outside the mainstream of the civilized world and for the most part had ignored them. This turned out to be a grave mistake. In the mid-fourth century B.C., just as Theban power was on the decline and exhaustion and confusion reigned in southern Greece, a brilliant and capable young man ascended the Macedonian throne. He was Philip II, who in an amazingly short time united the Macedonian tribes, forming a strong nation with a powerful army.

Eventually, Philip set his sights on making himself master of all the Greeks. Over the course of several years, he employed a highly effective combination of diplomacy, deceit, and naked aggression to seize large tracts of territory in northern and central Greece. In the summer of 338 B.C., accompanied by his eighteen-year-old son, Alexander (who would later be called "the Great"), he marched his army to Chaeronea, northwest of Thebes. There, the Macedonian forces clashed with those of a hastily organized coalition led by Athens and Thebes. In the face of Philip's superior strategy and tactics (some of them borrowed from Epaminondas), most of the allies eventually broke ranks and fled, Philip's victory was complete, and the Greek city-states now faced the dawn of a new political order.

After his win at Chaeronea, Philip attempted to create a confederacy of Greek states, in effect to unite the Greeks at last into a single political unit (although it was intended to be an alliance of small nations rather than a single large nation). In September 338, Philip presided over an assembly attended by delegates from many mainland and island city-states (the principal absentee being Sparta, which remained stubbornly aloof). "The Greek states were to make a common peace . . . with one another," noted classical historian Peter Green explains,

and constitute themselves into a federal Hellenic League. This league would take joint decisions by means of a federal council . . . on which each

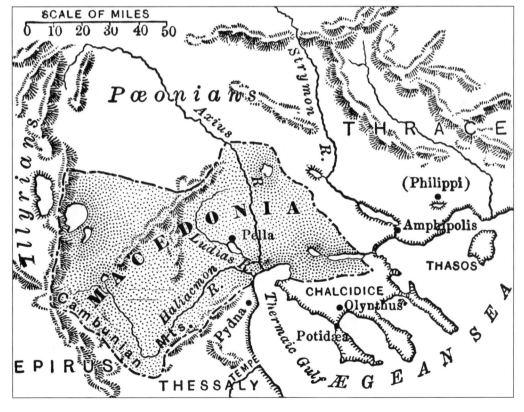

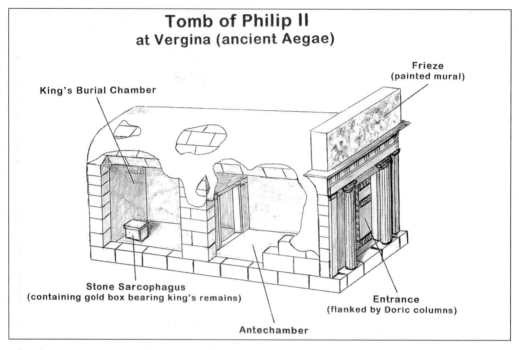

Tomb of Philip II
at Vergina (ancient Aegae)

Frieze
(painted mural)

King's Burial Chamber

Stone Sarcophagus
(containing gold box bearing king's remains)

Entrance
(flanked by Doric columns)

Antechamber

This drawing shows the main features of the tomb of Macedonia's King Philip II, discovered in the late 1970s by Greece's distinguished archaeologist, Manolis Andronikos.

state would be represented according to its size and military importance. . . . Simultaneously, the league was to form a separate alliance with Macedonia, though Macedonia itself would not be a member. This treaty was to be made with "Philip and his descendants" in perpetuity [forever]. The king would act as "leader" (hegemon) of the league's joint forces, a combined civil and military post designed to provide for the general security of Greece. [54]

The city-states also found themselves swept along in the tide of Philip's grandiose plans for invading Persia. In a twist of fate, however, in 336 a disgruntled Macedonian nobleman stabbed him to death in the small theater adjoining the royal palace at Aegae (in southern

Macedonia). Archaeologists have located and excavated this theater, as well as the palace itself.

A much more important discovery relating to Philip was made in 1977 by the noted Greek archaeologist Manolis Andronikos. Digging into a large mound at Vergina (the modern town built on the site of ancient Aegae), he found a tomb containing many finely made and valuable objects, including silver vessels and bronze armor. Among the artifacts was a gold box bearing a large star-burst, the characteristic symbol of the Macedonian kings. And inside the box, Andronikos found the cremated remains (including some bones and parts of the skull), of a man whom he identified as the great Philip himself. Although some scholars remain unconvinced, other evidence, albeit of an indirect nature, seems to support

EXPERTS EXAMINE THE SKULL UNEARTHED AT VERGINA

In this excerpt from his book *Making Faces: Using Forensic and Archaeological Evidence*, forensic expert Richard Neave describes how it was discovered that the skull found by archaeologist Manolis Andronikos in an ancient tomb at Vergina had suffered a blow to the eye. This was strong evidence for the theory that the skull belonged to Macedonia's renowned king Philip II.

"A layman looking at the broken and incomplete pieces of the skull sees only the cracks formed as the skull shrank in the heat of the fire [that had cremated the body]. . . . Striking though they are, these cracks have no pathological significance. What was significant to the eyes [of the surgeons consulted to examine the skull] was a small nick at the inner top corner of the right orbit, matched by a healed fracture of the cheek at the point where the two bones met. . . . There was even a small piece of bone missing at the suture. . . . To the surgeons, this showed that at some time well before his death this man had suffered a blow to the face that had left him blind in the right eye. . . . Suddenly, even before the reconstruction [of the man's face] . . . had begun, we had the answer that Andronikos had hoped for. Philip II's battle injuries are well known, for although the ancient authors tell us nothing about his physical appearance, there are many passages describing the wounds he received. . . . An Alexandrian academic of the first century B.C. called Didymus . . . says that Philip had his right eye cut out by an arrow during . . . the siege of Methone [on the northern Aegean coast]."

The gold funerary box (larnax) *bearing the remains of Philip II.*

his claim. In 1984 forensic scientist Richard Neave, working with surgical experts, studied the remains of the skull and determined that its owner had suffered a serious injury to the right eye. Ancient sources say that Philip suffered an eye injury when he was struck by an arrow while laying siege to a city.

Alexander and His Successors

With Philip removed from the picture, his ambitious and talented son ended up leading the expedition against Persia. In 334 B.C. Alexander crossed the Hellespont (the narrow strait separating northern Greece from Asia Minor) at the head of a small but, as it turned out, very formidable army. The first of his long series of victories and territorial gains occurred at the Granicus River, in northwestern Asia Minor, where he encountered an army commanded by some of the local Persian governors. In the following few years,

he twice defeated the Persian king Darius III; besieged and captured the island city of Tyre; liberated Egypt (which had been under Persian rule for two centuries) and there established a new city in the Nile Delta, naming it Alexandria after himself; occupied the three Persian capitals—Babylon, Susa, and Persepolis; and continued eastward, eventually reaching India. He may have gone on to further conquests. However, his exhausted troops, many of whom had not seen home and family in many years, mutinied and demanded that he turn back. This proved to be the end of the road for Alexander, for shortly after returning to Persia, he died, at the age of thirty-three, in Babylon on June 10, 323.

We have a fairly good idea of what this pivotal figure, Alexander, looked like, partly because a number of busts of him have survived. Although these tend to be somewhat idealized rather than strictly realistic, as

This section of the so-called "Alexander Mosaic," discovered in the House of the Faun in the Roman city of Pompeii, shows the Macedonian conqueror in the midst of battle.

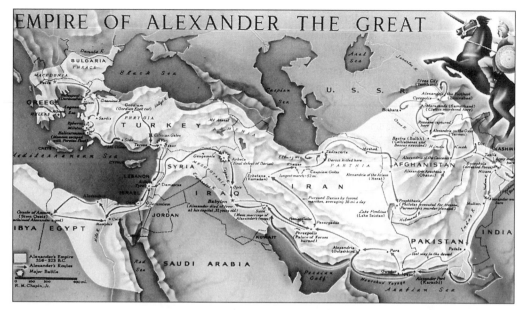

sculptures of kings and heroes tended to be at the time, they probably capture his basic features. Even more intriguing is another artistic depiction of Alexander brought to light by archaeologists, in this case a large mosaic scene found in the House of the Faun at Pompeii (the famous Roman town buried by a volcanic eruption in A.D. 79). Dubbed the "Alexander Mosaic," it depicts the climactic moment of one of the young conqueror's battles, probably Issus (333 B.C.), his first victory over Darius. "The elaborate and grandiose composition," writes William Biers,

> is centered on the two protagonists [leading characters], the bareheaded Alexander charging in from the left and the king [Darius] about to flee in his great chariot. Their eyes meet as Alexander runs through with his spear a Persian who has tried to block the way to his enemy. Another Persian offers his horse to the king as the charioteer fran-

tically tries to turn the unwieldly vehicle away from the encircling Greeks, whose spears can be seen behind the Persian horsemen. It is the moment of victory for the Macedonians.[55]

With a string of such victories, in just ten years Alexander had managed to conquer the vast Persian domain, in the process spreading Greek language, political administration, and culture to many parts of the Near East. But the huge kingdom he had created was immediately torn asunder as his leading generals and governors faced off and eventually came to death grips. Alexander's rightful heirs (a retarded half-brother; a son by his Persian wife, Roxane; and his mother, Olympias) were in time swept aside and murdered; and for the next forty-odd years, these men, who came to be called the "Successors" (*Diadochoi*), waged almost unrelenting war.

Finally, by about 280 B.C., three major new Greek kingdoms had emerged in the

A TINY FORCE MOVES A HUGE OBJECT

One of the greatest scientists of the Hellenistic Age (or any age) was Archimedes, who hailed from the Greek city of Syracuse. According to tradition, he bragged, "Give me place to stand on and I can move the world," a reference to his ongoing experiments with levers, with which he could use a tiny amount of force to move a huge object. Intrigued, Syracuse's king Hiero demanded a demonstration; and according to Plutarch's famous account (quoted in *Makers of Rome*):

"Archimedes chose for his demonstration a three-masted merchantman [cargo ship] of the royal fleet, which had been hauled ashore with immense labor by a large gang of men, and he proceeded to have the ship loaded with her usual freight and embarked a large number of passengers. He then seated himself at some distance away and without using any noticeable force, but merely exerting traction with his hand through a complex system of pulleys, he drew the vessel towards him with as smooth and even a motion as if she were gliding through the water."

eastern Mediterranean sphere. These so-called "successor-states" included the Ptolemaic Kingdom, founded by Ptolemy, consisting mainly of Egypt and parts of nearby Palestine; the Seleucid Kingdom, established by Seleucus, encompassing the lands north and west of the Persian Gulf—the heart of the old Persian Empire—and parts of Asia Minor; and the Macedonian Kingdom, created by Antigonus Gonatas, made up mostly of Macedonia and portions of the Greek mainland. Among the smaller but still influential states of the day were the kingdoms of Pergamum (in western Asia Minor) and Epirus (in extreme northwestern Greece); the Aetolian League (in western Greece) and Achaean League (in the Peloponnesus), federations of cities that had banded together for mutual protection; and some powerful independent city-states, notably the island of Rhodes (off the coast of Asia Minor) and Byzantium (on the Propontis, the waterway on the far side of the Hellespont).

The Hellenistic World

Historians refer to these realms as Hellenistic, meaning "Greek-like," since their societies often consisted of Eastern languages, customs, and ideas overlaid by a veneer of Greek ones. Likewise, the period lasting from Alexander's death in 323 B.C. to the death of the last Hellenistic ruler, Cleopatra VII, in 30 B.C., is called the Hellenistic Age. Historically speaking, this era was the last period of major Greek political independence in antiquity.

Yet its first century or so was a vigorous, prosperous period for the Greeks. And even as Greece's political decline proceeded, its artists and scientists continued to experiment and reach for new horizons; so that the age, as Michael Grant says, must not be viewed merely "as a sort of appendix of classical Greece. For [it] was rich and fertile in versatile creations which, despite all debts to the past, were very much its own."[56]

For example, Hellenistic Greek scientists—especially those working in Alexandria, which had become the known world's foremost commercial and intellectual center—made significant strides in anatomy, astronomy, and other fields. One of these men, Eratosthenes, correctly measured the earth's circumference to within one percent of the value accepted by modern science.[57]

This spirit of searching for the underlying truth of things found further expression in the arts, as poets, sculptors, and painters achieved levels of vividness and realism unknown in prior ages. The new spirit also generated, in Grant's words, "a greatly enhanced interest in the individual human being and his mind and emotions, an interest given vigorous expression by biographers and portrait artists."[58] A new style of sculpture, often called "psychological portraiture," is a prime example. In a statue or bust executed in this style, John Pedley explains,

the personality of the individual is revealed in the posture, set, and condition of the body, as well as in the facial expression. The desire to present a generic type (e.g., the philosopher, the king, or the orator) [a style common in the Classic Age] is replaced by an interest in representing

individual philosophers, kings, or orators.[59]

Interest in and concern for the individual also helped to improve the legal and social status and economic opportunities of women in many parts of the Hellenistic Greek world. Documents written on papyrus, mostly discovered in Egypt, show that women in that region (both Greek and native Egyptian) regularly gave and received loans; bought and sold land, slaves, and other property; inherited and bequeathed property and other legacies; and even made their own marriage contracts, perhaps sometimes without the consent of their fathers or other guardians.

Just as remarkable was the transformation of Greek society itself in Hellenistic times. Some scholars have suggested that Alexander dreamed of creating a sort of "world society," or "brotherhood of humanity," in which

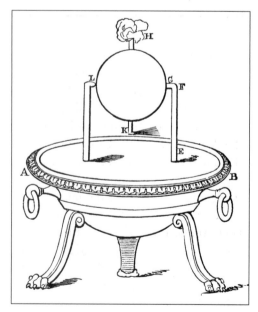

A reconstruction of the steam engine of Hero, a first-century A.D. *Greek inventor.*

all people under his rule, regardless of ancestry, would share a universal culture. Whether or not this accurately reflects his vision, what might be described as a modified version of such a society emerged in the eastern Mediterranean and Near East during the Hellenistic Age. This was the *oikoumene* (ee-koo-MEH-nee), or "inhabited world." Almost all of the Hellenistic realms, whether large or small, bore common political, economic, and cultural institutions that blended Greek and Near Eastern elements; so a traveler might feel more or less at home anywhere he or she went in the Hellenistic sphere.

The Same Fatal Mistake

It would be a mistake, however, to view this cultural blend, or Hellenistic society in general, as equal, fair, or classless. It was, in fact, a highly classist society that heavily favored Greeks, which is not surprising considering that Greeks established and controlled virtually all the states in the *oikoumene*. Greek Koine (a dialect that developed from the Attic, or Athenian, dialect) became the "lingua franca," the universal language of administration and business; and those who could not speak, read, and write Koine found it difficult, if not impossible, to get ahead in life. "In Alexandria, Antioch [in Syria], and the great Babylonian center of Seleucia-on-the-Tigris alike," remarks Chester Starr, "groups of relatively few Greeks constituted an upper crust much as did the English masters of Bombay, Singapore, or Hong Kong in the nineteenth century."[60] In his definitive study of the Hellenistic world, Peter Green elaborates:

> In all instances what the Successors set up were enclaves of Greco-Macedonian culture in an alien world, governmen-

tal ghettos for a ruling elite. When we come to assess the ubiquitous [existing seemingly everywhere] Greek temples, Greek theaters, Greek gymnasia, Greek mosaics, and Greek-language inscriptions scattered through the *oikoumene*, we should never forget that it was for the Hellenized Macedonian ruling minority and its Greek supporters . . . that such home-from-home luxuries . . . were . . . provided.[61]

One might assume that since the various Hellenistic rulers, aristocrats, and their supporters were all cut from the same cloth, so to speak, they would get along with one another. But the political reality of the era was exactly the opposite. The Hellenistic Greeks proceeded to repeat the same fatal mistake the city-states had; in short, they constantly argued and fought among themselves. The reasons for their disputes were many and complex. But the principal goal of the great monarchies, one that continually led to conflict, was to keep open and control the communication and travel lines to and from the Aegean Sea. This was partly to ensure a steady flow of Greek administrators, colonists, and mercenary (hired) soldiers from Greece. (Mercenaries were especially important, for all of the Hellenistic rulers used them in great numbers and the ready availability of "rent-an-army" generals became one of the chief hallmarks of the age.) It was also essential from an economic standpoint to have access to the Mediterranean ends of the great trade routes that ran west to east through the *oikoumene*; so when one ruler tried to monopolize those routes, one or more of the others moved to stop him.

Not surprisingly, the frequent bickering and warfare among the Hellenistic states inevitably reinforced their disunity and led to weakness and vulnerability to an outside power. In the mid-third century B.C., as they squabbled, oblivious to the potential consequences, far to the west that power—Rome—was rising steadily and ominously. In the next two centuries, the wings of the eagle (Rome's national symbol) would stretch outward, casting a mighty shadow over the known world and ultimately enfolding its peoples, including the Greeks.

CHAPTER SEVEN

FROM PYRRHUS TO CLEOPATRA: ROME ABSORBS THE GREEK LANDS

Throughout the fourth and third centuries B.C., the Greek city-states and kingdoms continued to bicker and fight among themselves. Moreover, except for Philip's and Alexander's brief attempt to create a confederacy of states, an effort that ultimately failed, the Greeks made no significant attempt to unite. This was bound to make them vulnerable to attack from outside the Greek sphere. And sure enough, in the second and first centuries B.C., Rome, master of the Italian peninsula, picked off the Greek states one by one and absorbed them into its expanding empire. It was the Romans, therefore, and not the Greeks, who subsequently went on to unite the whole Mediterranean world into a vast commonwealth administered by one central government.

The Romans Threaten the Italian Greeks

The Romans did not become a power capable of challenging the Greeks overnight. During the years that the Athenians were refining their democracy, erecting the Parthenon, and

fighting the Spartans for supremacy in Greece (i.e., the fifth century B.C.), Rome was still a small, relatively insignificant city-state nestled at the northern edge of the plain of Latium, near Italy's western coast. In the years that followed, in campaign after campaign launched by generation after generation, the Romans slowly but steadily expanded outward, conquering and absorbing their neighbors.

Inevitably, the Roman juggernaut rolled into southern Italy, a region largely dominated by Greek cities, many of them established as far back as the eighth and seventh centuries B.C. Greek habitation in the area was so dense that it came to be nicknamed Magna Graecia, meaning "Greater Greece." One of these cities, which the Romans called Metapontum, and the region surrounding it was a typical example. Located about eighteen miles from the Greek city of Taras, on the instep of the Italian "boot," Metapontum was by the late sixth century B.C. a prosperous city with streets laid out in an efficient grid pattern, several temples, its own silver coinage, and a network of outlying villages, farms, religious sanctuaries, and cemeteries. In recent years, the highly valuable archaeological technique of aerial photography has revealed over five hundred such minor sites in the first fifteen square miles of the city's outlying territory alone.[62]

In the early third century B.C. when the Romans began to threaten Magna Graecia, Metapontum, Taras (which the Romans called Tarentum), and the other Greek cities in the region were more sophisticated and culturally splendid than Rome. But none had armies that could credibly stand up to those fielded by the Romans. It is not surprising, therefore, that when Tarentum found itself at odds with Rome in the late 280s, it sent out an urgent call for aid to one of the most powerful Greek Hellenistic rulers of the day, Pyrrhus of Epirus.

The colorful and ambitious Pyrrhus answered this call. In crossing to Italy with his army in the spring of 280, he was likely motivated by more than just sympathy for fellow Greeks. His biographer, Plutarch, attributes the following remarks to him (which Pyrrhus may never have actually said, but which probably summarize what he was thinking at the time):

> If we can conquer the Romans, there is no other Greek or barbarian city which is a match for us. We shall straightaway become the masters of the whole of Italy. . . . After Italy, [we will take] Sicily, of course. . . . We can make it the spring-board for much greater enterprises. How could we resist making an attempt upon Libya and Carthage [both in North Africa]?[63]

Motivated by these dreams of conquest, Pyrrhus met the Romans in battle at Heraclea, not far from Tarentum, and scored a

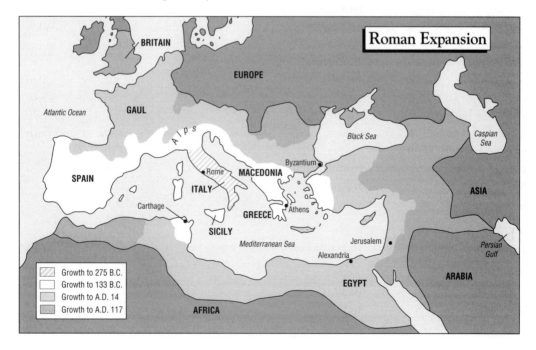

Pyrrhus, the famous third-century B.C. *Greek general who fought but could not decisively defeat the Romans.*

ous immediate consequences, namely that the Italian Greeks were now at the mercy of Rome, which by 265 was the undisputed master of all Italy. Pyrrhus's failure had additional, very ominous overtones. The fact that he, one of the greatest Greek generals of that or any day, could not decisively defeat the Romans did not bode well for Greece's future.

Greek and Roman Fighting Styles Compared

Before directly threatening the Greeks, however, the Romans tested the strength of their military machine against the powerful maritime empire of Carthage, centered in Tunisia (in North Africa). Just eleven years after Pyrrhus had vacated Italy, Rome engaged and defeated Carthage in the First Punic War (264–241 B.C.), the most destructive conflict the world had yet seen. The Second Punic War (218–202 B.C.) soon followed. In this truly stupendous conflict, Macedonia's king, Philip V made the mistake of allying himself with the ultimate loser—Carthage. (The Romans later referred to their involvement with him as the First Macedonian War, a subconflict of the greater war with Carthage.) And less than two years after their victory, the Romans were ready to punish Philip for his interference in their affairs. In this way, Rome, which had recently become master of the western Mediterranean sphere, now turned its attention to the Greek states in the sea's eastern sphere.

victory. But it was a costly one; for the Romans showed themselves to be stubborn and courageous fighters and slew some four thousand of Pyrrhus's men, over a sixth of his army. He fought the Romans again the following year at Ausculum, in southeastern Italy, and won again. But this time his losses were so great that he is said to have joked: "One more victory like that over the Romans will destroy us completely!"[64] Ever since, an excessively costly win has been called a "Pyrrhic victory."

After fighting still another costly battle against the Romans in 275 B.C., Pyrrhus decided to cut his losses and return to Epirus. The failure of his Italian adventure had seri-

Largely because these states remained disunited, their fates were virtually sealed. The so-called Second Macedonian War (200–197 B.C.) was noteworthy because it pitted the Mediterranean world's two most prestigious and feared military systems against each other. (Pyrrhus's battles with Rome had done the same, but because they had ended in a draw, more or less, they were seen as inconclusive.) The Greeks employed a unique battle formation known as the Macedonian phalanx, consisting of thousands of soldiers arrayed in ranks, one behind the other. Each man in the front rank held a battle pike (a long spear), and the men in the next few succeeding rear ranks held increasingly longer pikes, so that the tips projected outward from the front of the formation. The result was an impenetrable and frightening mass of spear points that resembled a giant porcupine with its quills erect. When this formation marched forward, it usually demolished all before it.

By contrast, Roman armies consisted of legions, groups of soldiers that in the era of the Second Punic War numbered between 4,000 and 5,000 each. On the battlefield, each legion broke down into smaller units called maniples, having from 60 to 120 men each, which could move around in various ways to form strategic patterns, the most common resembling a checkerboard. Each individual maniple or group of maniples was less formidable than a large Greek phalanx. Yet the Roman units could move back, forward, and around quickly at a commander's order, giving the Roman army a degree of flexibility that the stiff, monolithic phalanx lacked. According to the second-century B.C. Greek historian Polybius:

In a battle between Greeks and non-Greek tribesmen, a Greek phalanx crushes the opposition. Later, Philip II added progressively longer pikes, creating the dreaded Macedonian phalanx.

Nothing can withstand the frontal assault of the phalanx so long as it retains its characteristic formation and strength. What then is the factor which enables the Romans to win the battle and causes those who use the phalanx to fail? The answer is that . . . [the phalanx can only operate effectively on flat ground unencumbered by obstacles] . . . and [also that] the phalanx soldier cannot operate either in smaller units or singly, whereas the Roman formation is highly flexible. Every Roman soldier, once he . . . goes into action, can adapt himself equally well to any place or time and meet an attack from any quarter. [65]

Catastrophe at Cynoscephalae

Nowhere was this flexibility of the Roman soldier shown better than in the battle of Cynoscephalae ("Dog's Heads," fought in 197 B.C.), the final, decisive encounter of the Second Macedonian War. The outcome fully confirmed Polybius's astute analysis and showed that the Greek system, which had largely dominated Mediterranean land warfare for centuries, had become outmoded. The Macedonians were led by their king, Philip V, while the Roman commander was Titus Quinctius Flamininus. The two armies approached Cynoscephalae ridge (in Thessaly) and made camp, the Macedonians to the north, the Romans to the south. The next morning each commander, unaware of

THE TALENTED BUT SHORTSIGHTED PYRRHUS

This brief but insightful observation by Plutarch (quoted in *The Age of Alexander*), about the way the Epirote king Pyrrhus squandered his considerable talents and potential, could be applied just as fittingly to many of the other Hellenistic Greek rulers.

"Pyrrhus's hopes of the conquest of Italy and Sicily were finally demolished. He had squandered six years in his campaigns in these regions, but although he had been worsted in all his attempts, his spirit remained undaunted in the midst of defeat. The general opinion of him was that for warlike experience, daring, and personal valor, he had no equal among the kings of his time; but what he won through his feats of arms he lost by indulging in vain hopes, and through his obsessive desire to seize what lay beyond his grasp, he constantly failed to secure what lay within it. For this reason [he has been] compared to a player at dice, who makes many good throws, but does not understand how to exploit them when they are made."

In this scene carved on the famous column erected by the Roman emperor Trajan (which still stands), Roman legionaries march across a bridge constructed atop a row of boats.

the enemy's close proximity (mainly because fog blanketed the area), sent out a small covering force of skirmishers and horsemen to take control of the ridge. These forces ran into each other on the hill, a fight ensued, and in the coming hours it steadily escalated. "As the mist was clearing," noted ancient military historian Peter Connolly explains,

> both sides now decided to bring up the rest of their forces. The Romans were nearer to the pass and managed to deploy their forces while Philip was still bringing up his. Only his right wing [i.e., the right half of his phalanx] had

reached the top. . . . [His] cavalry and light-armed [troops], who were already engaged [with the Romans], were withdrawn and formed up on the right [of the phalanx]. Flamininus placed the elephants which were with his army in front of his right wing, told his troops there to stand fast, and advanced with his left wing. Philip . . . ordered [the members of] his phalanx to lower their spears and charge. . . . The charge of the phalanx drove the [Roman] legionaries back down the slope. Flamininus, seeing the imminent destruction of his left wing, threw himself at the head of the right wing and charged the Macedonian left wing, which was still forming up. The half-assembled Macedonian line crumbled before the onslaught of the elephants. . . . One of the tribunes [in the Roman right wing], seizing the initiative, took 20 maniples, . . . faced about, and charged . . . into the rear of the Macedonian right wing. The action was decisive; the phalanx, unable to turn, was cut to pieces. The Romans followed up their victory, cutting down the Macedonians where they stood, even though they raised their pikes to surrender.[66]

Philip's losses were some 8,000 killed and 5,000 captured, while the Romans lost only 700 men. In this single stroke, the Romans rendered the Greek military system obsolete and paved the way for Rome's absorption of the Greek lands in the ensuing decades.

A Dream of World Empire Shattered

Indeed, the results of the Greco-Roman battles and wars of those decades were hauntingly similar to that of Cynoscephalae. In 189 B.C., the Romans soundly defeated the ruler of the Seleucid Kingdom, Antiochus III, at Magnesia (in Asia Minor); the Third Macedonian War (171–168), against Philip V's son, Perseus, ended with the abolition of the Macedonian Kingdom and Rome's annexation of the area as a new province in 148; and in 146, after a courageous but futile military resistance by the Achaean League, the Romans brutally destroyed the once-great city of Corinth as an object lesson to other Greeks who might contemplate rebellion.

Meanwhile, the rulers of the Greek Ptolemaic Kingdom wisely submitted to Roman domination without a fight. For the next century, Egypt remained independent, but was in reality no more than a Roman client state (or vassal), allowed to pursue its own local affairs as long as it did Rome's bidding in the international scene. The Ptolemies of the first century B.C., who were weak, pale shadows of the formidable Greek general who had founded their dynasty, did their best to appease Rome and maintain their autonomy. But Egypt, with its vast stores of grain and royal treasure, increasingly became a prize coveted by the ambitious leading Romans of the day, who were vying for mastery of Rome's domains.

Cleopatra VII, daughter of King Ptolemy XII Auletes ("the Piper"), boldly allied herself with two of these leading Romans—Julius Caesar (who was assassinated in the Roman Senate in 44 B.C.) and Marcus Antonius (Mark Antony). For a while Antony and Cleopatra seemed on the verge of consolidating the whole East, including large portions of Alexander's former empire and the now-defunct Hellenistic monarchies. Had they succeeded, the course of Western history would undoubtedly have been quite different. As it was, however, a third powerful Roman, Octavian (later Augustus, the first Roman emperor), decisively defeated them at Actium (in western Greece), in 31 B.C. With her ally/lover dead and her dream of a world empire shattered, the famous queen—last of the Ptolemies, as well as the last Hellenistic ruler—committed suicide shortly afterward.

Back in 213 B.C., when the Romans were fighting Carthage and positioning themselves for Mediterranean mastery, a Greek

THE BATTLE OF ACTIUM

The Roman victory at the sea battle of Actium in 31 B.C. sounded the final death knell of large-scale Greek political autonomy in ancient times. This account of the opening moments of the battle is from the chronicle of Rome penned by the Romanized Greek historian Dio Cassius (ca. A.D. 163–ca. 235).

"At the sound of the trumpet Antony's fleet began to move, and, keeping close together, formed their line a little way outside the strait, but then advanced no further. Octavian moved out, as if to engage [the enemy]. . . . But when they neither came out against him, nor turned away . . . Octavian halted his advance, being in doubt as to what to do. He ordered his rowers to let their oars rest in the water, and waited for a while; after this he suddenly made a signal and, advancing both his wings [contingents on the far left and right], rounded his line in the form of an enveloping crescent. His object was to encircle the enemy if possible or, if not, at least to break up their formation. Antony was alarmed by this outflanking and encircling maneuver, moved forward to meet it as best he could, and so unwillingly joined battle with Octavian. So the fleets came to grips and the battle began. [The soldiers on the shore from] each side uttered loud shouts to the men aboard [the ships], urging the troops to summon up their prowess and their fighting spirit, and the men [on the ships] could also hear a babel of orders being shouted at them from those on shore."

This huge statue of Octavian was carved after he had become Augustus, the first Roman emperor.

orator, Agelaus of Aetolia, had recognized the potential danger and warned:

> It would be best of all if the Greeks never went to war with one another, if they could regard it as the greatest gift of the gods for them to speak with one voice, and could join hands like men who are crossing a river; in this way they could unite to repulse the incursions of the barbarians and to preserve themselves and their cities. [67]

At the time, the Hellenistic world's great powers could have and certainly should have joined forces, as Agelaus urged, and pre-sented a united front against the Roman threat. But his warning went unheeded.

So Cleopatra's death and Octavian's subsequent annexation of Egypt as part of the Roman Empire marked the end of large-scale independent Greek rule in antiquity. And for the next five centuries, Rome took Greece's place at the forefront of Western civilization. Pericles of Athens had been right about future ages standing in awe of the Greeks and their achievements. What he did not foresee was that the failure of his city and its neighbors to achieve lasting peace and unity would ensure that the leaders of those future ages would not be Greek.

THE
GREEK SPIRIT
LIVES ON

Under Roman rule, the Greeks retained many of their local customs and festivals, and daily life went on much as before. The degree of Greek assimilation into the greater Roman cultural melting pot varied from place to place and individual to individual. Some Greeks held themselves aloof and apart from Roman culture by not bothering to learn Latin and associating mainly with other Greeks. By contrast, other Greeks embraced the Roman system and the opportunities it afforded enterprising individuals. When possible they became Roman citizens, and a few managed to advance through the Roman ranks. Arrian, for example, the second-century A.D. Greek writer whose writings about Alexander the Great are the most complete surviving, became a Roman military leader and provincial governor.

For the Greek city-states and Greeks as a whole, however, forced entry into the Roman dominion had a serious disadvantage. Namely, they lost their long-cherished independence and with it the right to control their own destiny. As fate would have it, the Greeks would not taste political autonomy again until modern times (specifically, the 1830s, after a hard-fought war of independence from centuries of Turkish rule). Moreover, with the end of Greek democracy in the second century B.C., that enlightened form of government disappeared from the earth until the eighteenth century, when the American Revolution revived it in a new form.

But though Rome put an end to large-scale Greek political independence, it fortunately preserved much Greek culture; for the "Hellenization" of Rome proved far more profound and ultimately more influential than the "Romanization" of Greece. The highly practical Romans, who so often adopted the most attractive and useful aspects of the peoples they conquered, were greatly affected by Greek customs, arts, and ideas. In literature, architecture, painting, law, religion, philosophy, and numerous other areas, the Romans incorporated Greek styles and concepts, creating the Greco-Roman cultural fusion that eventually came to be called "classical" civilization. Later, in the Renaissance, many centuries after Rome's fall, Europe rediscovered classical culture, so much of which was based on Greek models. In this way, Greek democratic concepts, architectural wonders, and other cultural ideals came strongly to shape the modern Western world.

A Host of Greek Influences

Some of these Greek influences are obvious. Thousands of modern banks, government buildings, and other structures, for example, employ the familiar columns and triangular gables of classical Greek temple architecture. And every four years, most of the earth's nations, Western and non-Western alike, take part in the Olympic Games, inspired by and still featuring many of the same events of the original Greek version.

On the other hand, thousands of other aspects of Greek culture are so subtly interwoven into the very fabric of modern life that we are scarcely aware of their origins. Each time we attend the theater; or work out in a public gym; or compete on or watch a wrestling, boxing, or track and field team; or listen to a political speech; or go to the polls to vote; or formulate a political bill; or sue someone in court; or read a novel, essay, biography, or literary critique; or study or discuss philosophy; or contemplate atoms, the universe, or other scientific concepts; or attempt to solve problems using logic, we are doing things the Greeks invented over two millennia ago.

One of the simplest, yet also one of the noblest and most profound ideas the Greeks developed and passed on to future generations is the belief that the individual human being possesses innate dignity and worth. As C. M. Bowra puts it:

The imposing façade of the U.S. Supreme Court in Washington D.C., pictured here, employs many stylistic elements of classical Greek temple architecture.

At the center of the Greek outlook lay an unshakable belief in the worth of the individual man. In centuries when large parts of the earth were dominated by the absolute monarchies of the East, the Greeks were evolving their belief that a man must be respected not as an instrument of an omnipotent overlord, but for his own sake. . . . Nature nursed the Greeks in a hard school, but this made them conscious of themselves and their worth. Without this self-awareness, they would never have made their most important contribu-tion to human experience: the belief that a man must be honored for his individual worth and treated with re-spect just because he is himself. . . . This feeling among the Greeks may have started as something vague, but it was deeply felt, and it matured into reasoned philosophy which long after shaped, and still shapes, our own.[68]

Thus, though ancient Greek civilization was long ago lost in the physical sense, its unique and magnificent spirit lives on, helping in quiet but significant ways to guide our daily thoughts and actions.

NOTES

Introduction: How Do We Know About the Greeks?

1. Quoted in Sarah B. Pomeroy, *Goddesses, Whores, Wives, and Slaves: Women in Classical Antiquity*. New York: Schocken Books, 1995, p. 92.

2. John G. Pedley, *Greek Art and Archaeology*. New York: Harry N. Abrams, 1993, pp. 26–27.

Chapter 1: Palace-Fortresses and War-lords: Greece in the Bronze Age

3. Christopher Mee, "Minoan Crete," in Paul G. Bahn, ed., *The Cambridge Illustrated History of Archaeology*. New York: Cambridge University Press, 1996, pp. 147, 150.

4. J. Lesley Fitton, *The Discovery of the Greek Bronze Age*. Cambridge: Harvard University Press, 1996, pp.187–88.

5. For analyses of the various theories about Bronze Age migrations into Greece, see Robert Drews, *The Coming of the Greeks: Indo-European Conquests in the Aegean and Near East*. Princeton: Princeton University Press, 1988.

6. Sarah B. Pomeroy et al., *Ancient Greece: A Political, Social, and Cultural History*. New York: Oxford University Press, 1999, p. 10.

7. C. M. Bowra, *Classical Greece*. New York: Time-Life Books, 1965, pp. 31–32.

8. Pedley, *Greek Art and Archaeology*, p. 22.

9. Michael Grant, *The Rise of the Greeks*. New York: Macmillan, 1987, p. 147.

10. For an overview of these theories, see Robert Drews, *The End of the Bronze Age: Changes in Warfare and the Catastrophe of ca. 1200 B.C.* Princeton: Princeton University Press, 1993. Drews himself contends that military innovations among the peoples living on the periphery of the Mediterranean world allowed them to defeat the chariot corps of the Bronze Age kingdoms.

Chapter 2: The Greeks Reinvent Themselves: The Dark and Archaic Ages

11. William R. Biers, *The Archaeology of Greece*. Ithaca: Cornell University Press, 1996, p. 97.

12. Pomeroy et al., *Ancient Greece*, pp. 47–48.

13. Archaeologists have observed that some Athenian grave sites maintained a continuous series of similar-style burials from late Mycenaean times through the early Dark Age. This suggests an uninterrupted occupation of the area by people of the same culture.

14. Victor D. Hanson, *The Other Greeks: The Family Farm and the Agrarian Roots of Western Civilization*. New York: Simon & Schuster, 1995, p. 114.

15. Hanson, *Other Greeks*, p. 222.

16. Biers, *Archaeology of Greece*, pp. 127–28.

17. Quoted in Plutarch, *Life of Solon*, in *The Rise and Fall of Athens: Nine Greek Lives by Plutarch*, translated by Ian Scott-Kilvert. New York: Penguin, 1960, p. 60.

Chapter 3: The Classic Achievement: Athens's Cultural Golden Age

18. Chester G. Starr, *A History of the Ancient World*. New York: Oxford University Press, 1991, p. 275.

19. Michael Grant, *The Ancient Mediterranean*. New York: Penguin Books, 1969, p. 204.

20. Quoted in Thucydides, *The Peloponnesian War*, translated by Rex Warner. New York: Penguin Books, 1972, p. 148.

21. Herodotus, *The Histories*, translated by Aubrey de Sélincourt. New York: Penguin Books, 1972, p. 364.

22. Grant, *Rise of the Greeks*, p. 69.

23. In 499 B.C. the Ionian Greeks rebelled against the Persians and Athens sent the rebels aid. After crushing the rebellion in 494, Darius vowed to punish the Athenians for daring to meddle in his affairs.

24. W. G. Hardy, *The Greek and Roman World*. Cambridge, MA: Schenkman Publishing, 1962, p. 11.

25. Plutarch, *Life of Pericles*, in *Rise and Fall of Athens*, trans. Scott Kilvert, p. 177.

26. Plutarch, *Life of Pericles*, in *Rise and Fall of Athens*, trans. Scott-Kilvert, pp. 178–79.

27. John Miliadis, *The Acropolis*. Athens: M. Pechlivanidis, n.d., p. 52.

28. George D. Wilcoxon, *Athens Ascendant*. Ames: Iowa State University Press, 1979, p. 223.

29. Pausanias, *Guide to Greece*, 2 vols., translated by Peter Levi. New York: Penguin Books, 1971, vol. 1, pp. 469–71.

30. John Boardman, *The Parthenon and Its Sculptures*. Austin: University of Texas, 1985, p. 33.

31. Thomas Craven, *The Pocket Book of Greek Art*. New York: Pocket Books, 1950, pp. 95–96.

32. Another Athenian pottery style that gained popularity in the fifth century B.C. was the "white-ground" technique, in which figures were painted in delicate lines against a white background. White-ground paintings were most often used on the *lekythoi* placed in burial sites.

33. Biers, *Archaeology of Greece*, p. 335.

Chapter 4: Greek Society: Social Groups, Citizenship, and Political Institutions

34. N. R. E. Fisher, *Social Values in Classical Athens*. London: Dent, 1976, p. 5.

35. Fisher, *Social Values*, p. 9.

36. Herodotus, *Histories*, trans. Sélincourt, pp. 364–65.

37. Fisher, *Social Values*, p. 17.

38. Plutarch, *Life of Agis*, in *Plutarch on Sparta*, translated by Richard J. A. Talbert. New York: Penguin Books, 1988, p. 58.

39. The helots were originally the inhabitants of the neighboring region of Messenia. In the seventh century B.C., the Spartans conquered the Messenians and transformed them into serfs regulated by the state. In 464 B.C. these serfs rebelled, but the insurrection was brutally crushed. The helots' suffering finally ended in 369 B.C. when Thebes, which had decisively defeated Sparta two years before, invaded the Peloponnesus and set them free.

40. The first Athenian ostracism took place in 487 B.C. After 482 the procedure was employed only occasionally; and it fell into disuse after about 416. Some of the other Greek states that had forms of ostracism at various times were Argos (in the Peloponnesus), Megara (northwest of Athens), Miletus (in Ionia), and Syracuse (in Sicily).

41. Malcolm F. McGregor, *The Athenians and Their Empire*. Vancouver: University of British Columbia Press, 1987, p. 121.

42. Biers, *Archaeology of Greece*, pp. 21–22.

Chapter 5: Greek Society: Everyday Life, Customs, and Beliefs

43. Hanson, *Other Greeks*, p. 27.

44. Ian Jenkins, *Greek and Roman Life*. Cambridge: Harvard University Press, 1986, p. 5.

45. Pedley, *Greek Art and Archaeology*, pp. 285–86.

46. Cornelius Nepos, *The Book of the Great Generals of Foreign Nations*, translated by John Rolfe. Cambridge: Harvard University Press, 1960, p. 371.

47. Sue Blundell, *Women in Ancient Greece*. Cambridge: Harvard University Press, 1995, p. 151.

48. Blundell, *Women in Ancient Greece*, pp. 122–23.

49. Plutarch, *Life of Lycurgus*, in *Plutarch on Sparta*, trans. Talbert, pp. 25–26.

50. David Gill, "Classical Greece," in *Cambridge Illustrated History of Archaeology*, ed. Bahn, pp. 141–42.

Chapter 6: Incessant Rivalry and Disunity: The Ancient Greeks in Decline

51. Robert J. Littman, *The Greek Experiment: Imperialism and Social Conflict, 800–400 B.C.* London: Thames and Hudson, 1974, pp. 13–14, 20.

52. Thucydides, *The Peloponnesian War*, published as *The Landmark Thucydides: A Comprehensive Guide to the Peloponnesian War*, translated by Richard Crawley, edited by Robert B. Strassler. New York: Simon & Schuster, 1996, pp. 3, 93.

53. Xenophon, *Hellenica*, published as *A History of My Times*, translated by Rex Warner. New York: Penguin Books, 1979, p. 403.

54. Peter Green, *Alexander of Macedon, 356–323 B.C.: A Historical Biography*. Berkeley: University of California Press, 1991, p. 86.

55. Biers, *Archaeology of Greece*, p. 319.

56. Michael Grant, *From Alexander to Cleopatra: The Hellenistic World*. New

York: Charles Scribner's Sons, 1982, p. xiii.

57. Eratosthenes of Cyrene (ca. 276–194 B.C.) served for many years as the chief librarian of Alexandria's famous university, the Museum. For an account of how he measured the earth, as well as other achievements of Hellenistic scientists, see Don Nardo, *Greek and Roman Science*. San Diego: Lucent Books, 1997.

58. Grant, *From Alexander to Cleopatra*, p. xiii.

59. Pedley, *Greek Art and Archaeology*, pp. 330–31.

60. Starr, *History of the Ancient World*, p. 408.

61. Peter Green, *Alexander to Actium: The Historical Evolution of the Hellenistic Age*. Berkeley: University of California Press, 1990, p. 319.

Chapter 7: From Pyrrhus to Cleopatra: Rome Absorbs the Greek Lands

62. For more on archaeological studies of Greek settlements in southern Italy, see Pedley, *Greek Art and Archaeology*, pp. 292–93; and Michael Grant, *The Visible Past: Recent Archaeological Discoveries of Greek and Roman History*. New York: Scribner's, 1990, pp. 15–19, 63–66.

63. Plutarch, *Life of Pyrrhus*, in *The Age of Alexander: Nine Greek Lives by Plutarch*, translated by Ian Scott-Kilvert. New York: Penguin Books, 1973, p. 399.

64. Plutarch, *Life of Pyrrhus*, in *Age of Alexander*, trans. Scott-Kilvert, p. 409.

65. Polybius, *Histories*, published as Polybius: *The Rise of the Roman Empire*, translated by Ian Scott-Kilvert. New York: Penguin Books, 1979, pp. 511–13.

66. Peter Connolly, *Greece and Rome at War*. London: Greenhill Books, 1998, pp. 205–206.

67. Quoted in Polybius, *Histories*, trans. Scott-Kilvert, pp. 299–300.

Epilogue: The Greek Spirit Lives On

68. C. M. Bowra, *Classical Greece*, pp. 11–12.

CHRONOLOGY

B.C.

ca. 3000–ca. 1100

Greece's Bronze Age, in which people use tools and weapons made of bronze.

ca. 2000 (or possibly somewhat later)

Tribal peoples speaking an early form of Greek begin entering the Greek peninsula from the east or northeast; their descendants, whom scholars refer to as Mycenaeans, spread across mainland Greece.

ca. 1500–ca. 1400

Mycenaean warlords overthrow another early Aegean people, the Minoans, who have long controlled Crete.

ca. 1200–ca. 1100

For reasons still unclear, the Mycenaean kingdoms and fortresses suffer widespread destruction and rapidly decline.

ca. 1100–ca. 800

Greece's Dark Age, in which poverty and illiteracy are at first widespread and about which modern scholars know very little.

ca. 850–ca. 750

The most likely period in which the legendary epic poet Homer lived and composed the *Iliad* and *Odyssey*.

ca. 800–ca. 500

Greece's Archaic Age, characterized by the rise of city-states, the return of prosperity and literacy, rapid population growth, and intensive colonization of the Mediterranean and Black Seas.

776

Traditional date for the first Olympic Games, held at Olympia, in the northwestern Peloponnesus.

594

The Athenians charge a prominent citizen named Solon with the task of revising Athens's social and political system.

ca. 508

Building on Solon's reforms, an aristocrat named Cleisthenes and his supporters transform Athens's government into the world's first democracy.

ca. 500–323

Greece's Classic Age, in which Greek arts, architecture, literature, and democratic reforms reach their height.

490

The Persian ruler Darius sends an expedition to sack Athens, but the Athenians decisively defeat the invaders at Marathon (northeast of Athens).

480

Darius's son, Xerxes, launches a massive invasion of Greece; the Greeks win a series of stunning victories and in the following year expel the Persians from the Aegean sphere.

461

In Athens a leading democratic politician named Pericles becomes the city's most influential leader.

447

Construction begins on a major new temple complex atop Athens's Acropolis; nine years later, the magnificent Parthenon temple is dedicated to the goddess Athena.

431

Sparta declares war on Athens, initiating the disastrous Peloponnesian War, which engulfs and exhausts almost all the city-states.

404

Athens surrenders, ending the great war and initiating a Spartan hegemony (domination) of Greece.

371

The Theban leader Epaminondas defeats the Spartans at Leuctra (near Thebes) and soon afterward invades the Peloponnesus, initiating a period of Theban hegemony.

359

King Philip II takes charge of the disunited, culturally backward kingdom of Macedonia and soon begins to forge Europe's first national standing army.

338

Philip and his teenaged son, Alexander (who will later be called "the Great"), defeat an alliance of city-states at Chaeronea (near Thebes).

334–323

After Philip's assassination, Alexander invades Persia, carves out the largest empire the world has yet seen, and dies in the Persian capital of Babylon.

323–30

Greece's Hellenistic Age, in which Alexander's generals, the so-called "Successors," war among themselves and carve up his empire into several new kingdoms, which then proceed also to fight among themselves; during the second half of this period, Rome gains control of the Greek world.

ca. 280

Three large Greek monarchies (the Macedonian, Seleucid, and Ptolemaic Kingdoms) have by now emerged from the chaos of the long wars of the Successors.

200–197

Rome prosecutes and wins the Second Macedonian War against Macedonia's king Philip V.

171–168

Rome wins the Third Macedonian War against Philip's son, Perseus, and dismantles the Macedonian Kingdom.

146

A Roman general destroys the once-great Greek city of Corinth as an object lesson to any Greeks contemplating rebellion against Rome.

31

The Roman leader Octavian (the future emperor Augustus) defeats the Roman general Mark Antony and Greek queen of Egypt, Cleopatra, at Actium (in western Greece); the following year, the legendary queen, last of the Hellenistic and major autonomous Greek rulers of antiquity, takes her own life.

For Further Reading

Isaac Asimov, *The Greeks: A Great Adventure*. Boston: Houghton Mifflin, 1965. An excellent, entertaining overview of Greek history and culture.

David Bellingham, *An Introduction to Greek Mythology*. Secaucus, NJ: Chartwell Books, 1989. Explains the major Greek myths and legends and their importance to the ancient Greeks. Contains many beautiful photos and drawings.

C. M. Bowra, *Classical Greece*. New York: Time-Life Books, 1965. Despite the passage of more than thirty years, this volume—written by a renowned classical historian and adorned with numerous maps, drawings, and color photos—is only slightly dated and remains one of the best introductions to ancient Greece for general readers.

Peter Connolly, *The Greek Armies*. Morristown, NJ: Silver Burdette, 1979. A fine, detailed study of Greek armor, weapons, and battle tactics, filled with colorful, accurate illustrations by Connolly, the world's leading artistic interpreter of the ancient world. Highly recommended.

Denise Dersin, *Greece: Temples, Tombs, and Treasures*. Alexandria, VA: Time-Life Books, 1994. In a way a newer companion volume to Bowra's book (see above), this is also excellent and features a long, up-to-date, and beautifully illustrated chapter on Athens's golden age.

Rhoda A. Hendricks, trans., *Classical Gods and Heroes*. New York: Morrow Quill, 1974. A collection of easy-to-read translations of famous Greek myths and tales, as told by ancient Greek and Roman writers, including Homer, Hesiod, Pindar, Apollodorus, Ovid, and Virgil.

Susan Peach and Anne Millard, *The Greeks*. London: Usborne, 1990. A general overview of the history, culture, myths, and everyday life of ancient Greece, presented in a format suitable to young, basic readers (although the many fine, accurate color illustrations make the book appealing to anyone interested in ancient Greece).

Jonathon Rutland, *See Inside an Ancient Greek Town*. New York: Barnes and Noble, 1995. This colorful introduction to ancient Greek life is aimed at basic readers.

John Warry, *Warfare in the Classical World*. Norman: University of Oklahoma Press, 1980, 1995. A beautifully mounted book filled with accurate and useful paintings, drawings, maps, and diagrams. The text is also first rate, providing much detailed information about the weapons, clothing, strategies, battle tactics, and military leaders of the Greeks, Romans, and the peoples they fought.

Author's Note:

In the following volumes, I provide much useful background information about Greek history and culture, including the Greek-Persian conflict; the rise and fall of the Athenian empire; the golden age of arts, literature, and architecture; and sketches of the important Greek politicians, military leaders, writers, and artists. Though they are aimed at high school readers, the high level of detail and documentation in these volumes make then useful for older general readers as well.

Don Nardo, *The Age of Pericles*. San Diego: Lucent Books, 1995.

———, *Greek and Roman Sport*. San Diego: Lucent Books, 1999.

———, *Greek and Roman Theater*. San Diego: Lucent Books, 1995.

———, *Leaders of Ancient Greece*. San Diego: Lucent Books, 1999.

———, *Life in Ancient Athens*. San Diego: Lucent Books, 2000.

———, *The Parthenon*. San Diego: Lucent Books, 1999.

———, *The Trial of Socrates*. San Diego: Lucent Books, 1997.

WORKS CONSULTED

Ancient Sources:

Aeschylus, *The Persians*, in *Aeschylus: Prometheus Bound, The Suppliants, Seven Against Thebes, The Persians*. Translated by Philip Vellacott. Baltimore: Penguin Books, 1961; and the *Oresteia*, published as *The Orestes Plays of Aeschylus*. Translated by Paul Roche. New York: New American Library, 1962.

Kenneth J. Atchity, ed., *The Classical Greek Reader*. New York: Oxford University Press, 1996. A collection of translations of ancient Greek writings, including those of Homer, Solon, Herodotus, Lysias, Xenophon, Aristotle, Sophocles, Demosthenes, and many others.

Diodorus Siculus, *Library of History* (or *Universal History*). 12 vols. Translated by Charles L. Sherman and C. Bradford Welles. Cambridge: Harvard University Press, 1963.

Herodotus, *The Histories*. Translated by Aubrey de Sélincourt. New York: Penguin Books, 1972.

Cornelius Nepos, *The Book of the Great Generals of Foreign Nations*. Translated by John Rolfe. Cambridge: Harvard University Press, 1960.

Pausanias, *Guide to Greece*. 2 vols. Translated by Peter Levi. New York: Penguin Books, 1971.

Pindar, *Odes*. Translated by C. M. Bowra. New York: Penguin Books, 1969.

Plato, *Dialogues*, in *The Dialogues of Plato*. Translated by Benjamin Jowett. Great Books. Chicago: Encyclopedia Britannica, 1952.

Plutarch, *Parallel Lives*, excerpted in *The Rise and Fall of Athens: Nine Greek Lives by Plutarch*. Translated by Ian Scott-Kilvert. New York: Penguin Books, 1960; also excerpted in *The Age of Alexander: Nine Greek Lives by Plutarch*. Translated by Ian Scott-Kilvert. New York: Penguin Books, 1973; and *Plutarch: Makers of*

Rome. Translated by Ian Scott-Kilvert. New York: Penguin Books, 1965.

————, *Parallel Lives* and *Moralia (Moral Essays)*, excerpted in *Plutarch On Sparta*. Translated by Richard J. A. Talbert. New York: Penguin Books, 1988.

J. J. Pollitt, ed. and trans., *The Art of Ancient Greece: Sources and Documents*. New York: Cambridge University Press, 1990. A compilation of translations of ancient sources dealing with painting, sculpture, architecture, and other artistic genres.

Polybius, *Histories*, published as *Polybius: The Rise of the Roman Empire*. Translated by Ian Scott-Kilvert. New York: Penguin Books, 1979.

Waldo E. Sweet, ed., *Sport and Recreation in Ancient Greece: A Sourcebook with Translations*. New York: Oxford University Press, 1987. A collection of translations of ancient sources describing sports, games, music, dance, theater, and related leisure activities.

Thucydides, *The Peloponnesian War*. Translated by Rex Warner. New York: Penguin Books, 1972; and also published as *The Landmark Thucydides: A Comprehensive Guide to the Peloponnesian War*. Translated by Richard Crawley, edited by Robert B. Strassler. New York: Simon & Schuster, 1996.

Thomas Wiedemann, ed., *Greek and Roman Slavery*. Baltimore: Johns Hopkins University Press, 1981. A compilation of translations of ancient sources dealing with slavery.

Xenophon, *Hellenica*, published as *A History of My Times*. Translated by Rex Warner. New York: Penguin Books, 1979.

————, *Memorabilia and Oeconomicus*. Translated by E. C. Marchant. Cambridge: Harvard University Press, 1965.

Modern Sources:

Archaeological Rediscovery of Greece

Paul G. Bahn, ed., *The Cambridge Illustrated History of Archaeology*. New York: Cambridge University Press, 1996.

William R. Biers, *The Archaeology of Greece*. Ithaca: Cornell University Press, 1996.

J. Lesley Fitton, *The Discovery of the Greek Bronze Age*. Cambridge: Harvard University Press, 1996.

Michael Grant, *The Visible Past: Recent Archaeological Discoveries of Greek and Roman History*. New York: Scribner's, 1990.

Paul MacKendrick, *The Greek Stones Speak: The Story of Archaeology in Greek Lands*. New York: W. W. Norton, 1962.

Richard Neave and John Prag, *Making Faces: Using Forensic and Archaeological Evidence*. College Station: Texas A&M University Press, 1997.

Michael Shanks, *The Classical Archaeology of Greece*. London: Routledge, 1995.

Anthony M. Snodgrass, *An Archaeology of Greece*. Berkeley: University of California Press, 1987.

Fani-Maria Tsigakou, *The Rediscovery of Greece: Travelers and Painters of the Romantic Era*. London: Thames and Hudson, 1981.

A. G. Woodhead, *The Study of Greek Inscriptions*. London: Bristol Classical Press, 1992.

Architecture, Engineering, and Athenian Acropolis Complex

Manolis Andronikos, *The Acropolis*. Athens: Ekdotike Athenon, 1994.

John Boardman, *The Parthenon and Its Sculptures*. Austin: University of Texas, 1985.

Vincent J. Bruno, ed., *The Parthenon*. New York: Norton, 1974.

L. Sprague de Camp, *The Ancient Engineers*. New York: Ballantine Books, 1963.

Peter Green, *The Parthenon*. New York: Newsweek Book Division, 1973.

Ian Jenkins, *The Parthenon Frieze*. Austin: University of Texas, 1994.

John Miliadis, *The Acropolis*. Athens: M. Pechlivanidis, n.d.

A. W. Lawrence, *Greek Architecture*. Revised by R. A. Tomlinson. New Haven: Yale University Press, 1996.

Panayotis Tournikiotis, ed., *The Parthenon and Its Impact in Modern Times*. New York: Harry N. Abrams, 1996.

R. E. Wycherly, *The Stones of Athens*. Princeton: Princeton University Press, 1978.

Art and Sculpture

Carl Bluemel, *Greek Sculptors at Work*. London: Phaidon, 1969.

John Boardman, *Greek Art*. New York: Praeger, 1964.

———, ed., *The Oxford History of Classical Art*. Oxford: Oxford University Press, 1993.

Thomas Craven, *The Pocket Book of Greek Art*. New York: Pocket Books, 1950.

John G. Pedley, *Greek Art and Archaeology*. New York: Harry N. Abrams, 1993.

Nigel Spivey, *Greek Art*. London: Phaidon, 1997.

General Ancient Greek History, Geography, and Culture

Lesly Adkins and Roy A. Adkins, *Handbook to Life in Ancient Greece*. New York: Facts On File, 1997.

C. M. Bowra, *Classical Greece*. New York: Time-Life Books, 1965.

———, *The Greek Experience*. New York: New American Library, 1957.

J. B. Bury, *A History of Greece to the Death of Alexander*. Revised by Russell Meiggs. London: Macmillan, 1975.

John A. Crow, *Greece: The Magic Spring*. New York: Harper & Row, 1970.

Victor Ehrenberg, *From Solon to Socrates: Greek History and Civilization During the 6th and 5th Centuries* B.C. London: Methuen, 1967.

M. I. Finley, *The Ancient Greeks: An Introduction to Their Life and Thought*. New York: Viking Press, 1964.

Charles Freeman, *Egypt, Greece, and Rome: Civilizations of the Ancient Mediterranean*. New York: Oxford University Press, 1996.

Michael Grant, *The Ancient Mediterranean*. New York: Penguin Books, 1969.

———, *The Classical Greeks*. New York: Scribner's, 1989.

———, *The Founders of the Western World: A History of Greece and Rome*. New York: Scribner's, 1991.

————, *A Guide to the Ancient World.* New York: Barnes and Noble, 1996.

————, *The Rise of the Greeks.* New York: Macmillan, 1987.

W. G. Hardy, *The Greek and Roman World.* Cambridge, MA: Schenkman Publishing, 1962.

Ian Jenkins, *Greek and Roman Life.* Cambridge: Harvard University Press, 1986.

Peter Levi, *Atlas of the Greek World.* New York: Facts On File, 1984.

Thomas R. Martin, *Ancient Greece: From Prehistoric to Hellenistic Times.* New Haven: Yale University Press, 1996.

Malcolm F. McGregor, *The Athenians and Their Empire.* Vancouver: University of British Columbia Press, 1987.

Christian Meier, *Athens: Portrait of a City in Its Golden Age.* Translated by Robert and Rita Kimber. New York: Henry Holt, 1998.

Sarah B. Pomeroy et al., *Ancient Greece: A Political, Social, and Cultural History.* New York: Oxford University Press, 1999.

C. E. Robinson, *Everyday Life in Ancient Greece.* Oxford: Clarendon Press, 1968.

Chester G. Starr, *The Ancient Greeks.* New York: Oxford University Press, 1971.

————, *A History of the Ancient World.* New York: Oxford University Press, 1991.

Richard J. A. Talbert, ed., *Atlas of Classical History.* London: Routledge, 1985.

George D. Wilcoxon, *Athens Ascendant.* Ames: Iowa State University Press, 1979.

Gods, Myths, Worship, Burial Customs, and Religious Festivals

Walter Burkert, *Greek Religion, Archaic and Classical.* Oxford: Basil Blackwell, 1985.

Robert Garland, *The Greek Way of Death.* Ithaca: Cornell University Press, 1985.

Michael Grant, *Myths of the Greeks and Romans.* New York: Penguin Books, 1962.

Evi Melas, *Temples and Sanctuaries of Ancient Greece.* London: Thames and Hudson, 1973.

John D. Mikalson, *Athenian Popular Religion.* Chapel Hill: University of North Carolina Press, 1983.

Mark P. O. Morford and Robert J. Lenardon, *Classical Mythology.* New York: Longmans, 1985.

Jennifer Neils, *Goddess and Polis: The Panathenaic Festival in Ancient Athens.* Princeton: Princeton University Press, 1992.

Hellenistic Age and Its Culture

John Boardman et al., *Greece and the Hellenistic World.* New York: Oxford University Press, 1988.

Max Cary, *History of the Greek World from 323 to 146* B.C. London: Methuen, 1968.

Michael Grant, *From Alexander to Cleopatra: The Hellenistic World.* New York: Charles Scribner's Sons, 1982.

Peter Green, *Alexander to Actium: The Historical Evolution of the Hellenistic Age.* Berkeley: University of California Press, 1990.

————, ed., *Hellenistic History and Culture.* Berkeley: University of California Press, 1993.

Naphtali Lewis, *Greeks in Ptolemaic Egypt.* Oxford: Clarendon Press, 1986.

————, *Life in Egypt Under Roman Rule.* Oxford: Clarendon Press, 1983.

Don Nardo, *Greek and Roman Science.* San Diego: Lucent Books, 1997.

————, ed., *The Decline and Fall of Ancient Greece.* San Diego: Greenhaven Press, 2000.

J. J. Pollitt, *Art in the Hellenistic Age.* Cambridge: Cambridge University Press, 1986.

Sarah B. Pomeroy, *Women in Hellenistic Egypt: From Alexander to Cleopatra.* New York: Schocken Books, 1989.

F. W. Walbank, *The Hellenistic World.* Cambridge: Harvard University Press, 1993.

Literature, Theater, Philosophy, and Ideas

H. C. Baldry, *The Greek Tragic Theater*. New York: W. W. Norton, 1971.

C. M. Bowra, *Homer*. New York: Scribner's, 1972.

James H. Butler, *The Theater and Drama of Greece and Rome*. San Francisco: Chandler Publishing, 1972.

Lionel Casson, *Masters of Ancient Comedy*. New York: Macmillan, 1960.

E. R. Dodds, *The Greeks and the Irrational*. Berkeley: University of California Press, 1968.

Michael Grant, *Greek and Roman Historians: Information and Misinformation*. London: Routledge, 1995.

Victor D. Hanson and John Heath, *Who Killed Homer?: The Demise of Classical Education and the Recovery of Greek Wisdom*. New York: Free Press, 1998.

Peter Levi, *A History of Greek Literature*. New York: Viking, 1985.

Don Nardo, ed., *Greek Drama*. San Diego: Greenhaven Press, 2000.

———, ed., *Readings on Homer*. San Diego: Greenhaven Press, 1998.

———, ed., *Readings on Sophocles*. San Diego: Greenhaven Press, 1997.

Rex Warner, *The Greek Philosophers*. New York: New American Library, 1958.

Politics, Democracy, Citizenship, and Legal Institutions

David Cohen, *Law, Violence, and Community in Classical Athens*. New York: Cambridge University Press, 1995.

J. K. Davies, *Democracy and Classical Greece*. Cambridge: Harvard University Press, 1993.

Kathleen Freeman, *The Murder of Herodes and Other Trials from the Athenian Law Courts*. New York: W. W. Norton, 1963.

Douglas M. MacDowell, *The Law in Classical Athens*. Ithaca: Cornell University Press, 1978.

Alfred Zimmern, *The Greek Commonwealth: Politics and Economics in Fifth-Century Athens*. 5th ed. 1931. Revised and reprinted, New York: Oxford University Press, 1961.

Prominent Ancient Greek Figures

J. K. Anderson, *Xenophon*. New York: Scribner's, 1974.

Jonathon Barnes, *Aristotle*. New York: Oxford University Press, 1982.

J. A. S. Evans, *Herodotus*. Boston: Twayne Publishers, 1982.

Kathleen Freeman, *The Work and Life of Solon, with a Translation of His Poems*. Cardiff: University of Wales Press, 1926. Reprint, New York: Arno, 1976.

J. F. C. Fuller, *The Generalship of Alexander the Great*. New Brunswick, NJ: Rutgers University Press, 1960.

Michael Grant, *The Classical Greeks*. New York: Scribner's, 1989.

Peter Green, *Alexander of Macedon, 356–323 B.C.: A Historical Biography*. Berkeley: University of California Press, 1991.

N. G. L. Hammond, *The Genius of Alexander the Great*. Chapel Hill: University of North Carolina Press, 1997.

———, *Philip of Macedon*. Baltimore: Johns Hopkins University Press, 1994.

R. M. Hare, *Plato*. New York: Oxford University Press, 1982.

Lucy Hughes-Hallett, *Cleopatra: Histories, Dreams and Distortions*. New York: HarperCollins, 1991.

Donald Kagan, *Pericles of Athens and the Birth of Democracy*. New York: Free Press, 1991.

Robert B. Kebric, *Greek People*. Mountain View, CA: Mayfield Publishing, 1997.

Don Nardo, ed., *Cleopatra*. San Diego: Greenhaven Press, 2000.

———, *Philip II and Alexander the Great Unify Greece*. Springfield, NJ: Enslow Publishers, 2000.

A. J. Podlecki, *The Life of Themistocles*. Montreal: McGill-Queen's University Press, 1975.

A. E. Taylor, *Socrates: The Man and His Thought*. New York: Doubleday, 1952.

Social Institutions and Customs

Sue Blundell, *Women in Ancient Greece*. Cambridge: Harvard University Press, 1995.

James Davidson, *Courtesans and Fishcakes: The Consuming Passions of Classical Athens*. New York: St. Martin's Press, 1998.

Victor Ehrenberg, *The People of Aristophanes: A Sociology of Old Attic Comedy*. New York: Schocken Books, 1962.

N. R. E. Fisher, *Social Values in Classical Athens*. London: Dent, 1976.

Robert Garland, *The Greek Way of Life*. Ithaca: Cornell University Press, 1990.

Mark Golden, *Children and Childhood in Classical Athens*. Baltimore: Johns Hopkins University Press, 1990.

Victor D. Hanson, *The Other Greeks: The Family Farm and the Agrarian Roots of Western Civilization*. New York: Simon & Schuster, 1995.

Robert J. Littman, *The Greek Experiment: Imperialism and Social Conflict, 800–400 B.C.* London: Thames and Hudson, 1974.

Sarah B. Pomeroy, *Goddesses, Whores, Wives, and Slaves: Women in Classical Antiquity*. New York: Schocken Books, 1995.

Sports and Games

M. I. Finley and H. W. Pleket, *The Olympic Games: The First Thousand Years*. New York: Viking Press, 1976.

Vera Olivova, *Sports and Games in the Ancient World*. New York: St. Martin's Press, 1984.

David Sansone, *Greek Athletics and the Genesis of Sport*. Berkeley: University of California Press, 1988.

Judith Swaddling, *The Ancient Olympic Games*. 1980. Reprinted, Austin: University of Texas Press, 1996.

D. C. Young, *The Olympic Myth of Greek Amateur Athletics*. Chicago: Ares, 1984.

War, Weapons, and Military Customs and Tactics

F. E. Adcock, *The Greek and Macedonian Art of War*. Berkeley: University of California Press, 1957.

Peter Connolly, *Greece and Rome at War*. London: Greenhill Books, 1998.

Peter Green, *The Greco-Persian Wars*. Berkeley: University of California Press, 1996.

Sir John Hackett, ed., *Warfare in the Ancient World*. New York: Facts On File, 1989.

Victor D. Hanson, *The Wars of the Ancient Greeks*. London: Cassell, 1999.

————, *The Western Way of War: Infantry Battle in Classical Greece*. New York: Oxford University Press, 1989.

Donald Kagan, *The Outbreak of the Peloponnesian War*. Ithaca: Cornell University Press, 1969.

John Lazenby, *The Defense of Greece*. Bloomington, IL: David Brown, 1993.

John Warry, *Warfare in the Classical World*. Norman: University of Oklahoma Press, 1995.

INDEX

PICTURE CREDITS

ABOUT THE AUTHOR

Historian Don Nardo has written numerous volumes about the ancient Greek world, including *The Age of Pericles*, *Greek and Roman Sport*, *The Parthenon*, and *Life in Ancient Athens*. He is also the editor of *The Decline and Fall of Ancient Greece*, Greenhaven Press's *The Complete History of Ancient Greece*, and literary companions to the works of Homer and Sophocles. Along with his wife, Christine, he resides in Massachusetts.